Easter Bunny
COLORING BOOK
By Piggyback Press

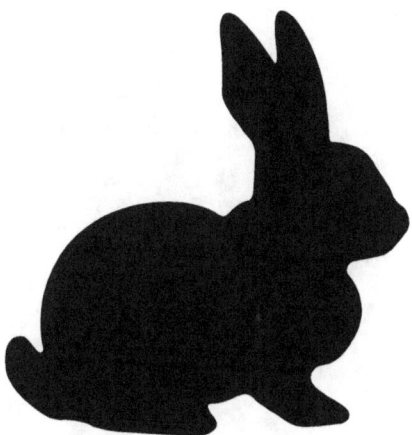

COLORING TIP:

You might find that the spine of the book might get in the way of you coloring. My suggestion is to cut out each design so that you work on a flat surface. If you are using colored markers or even water color, I would also suggest to have scrap paper beneath you coloring sheets. **Happy Spring! Happy Easter and happy coloring!**

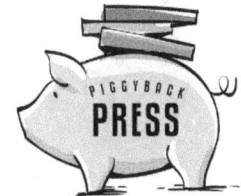

piggybackpress.com

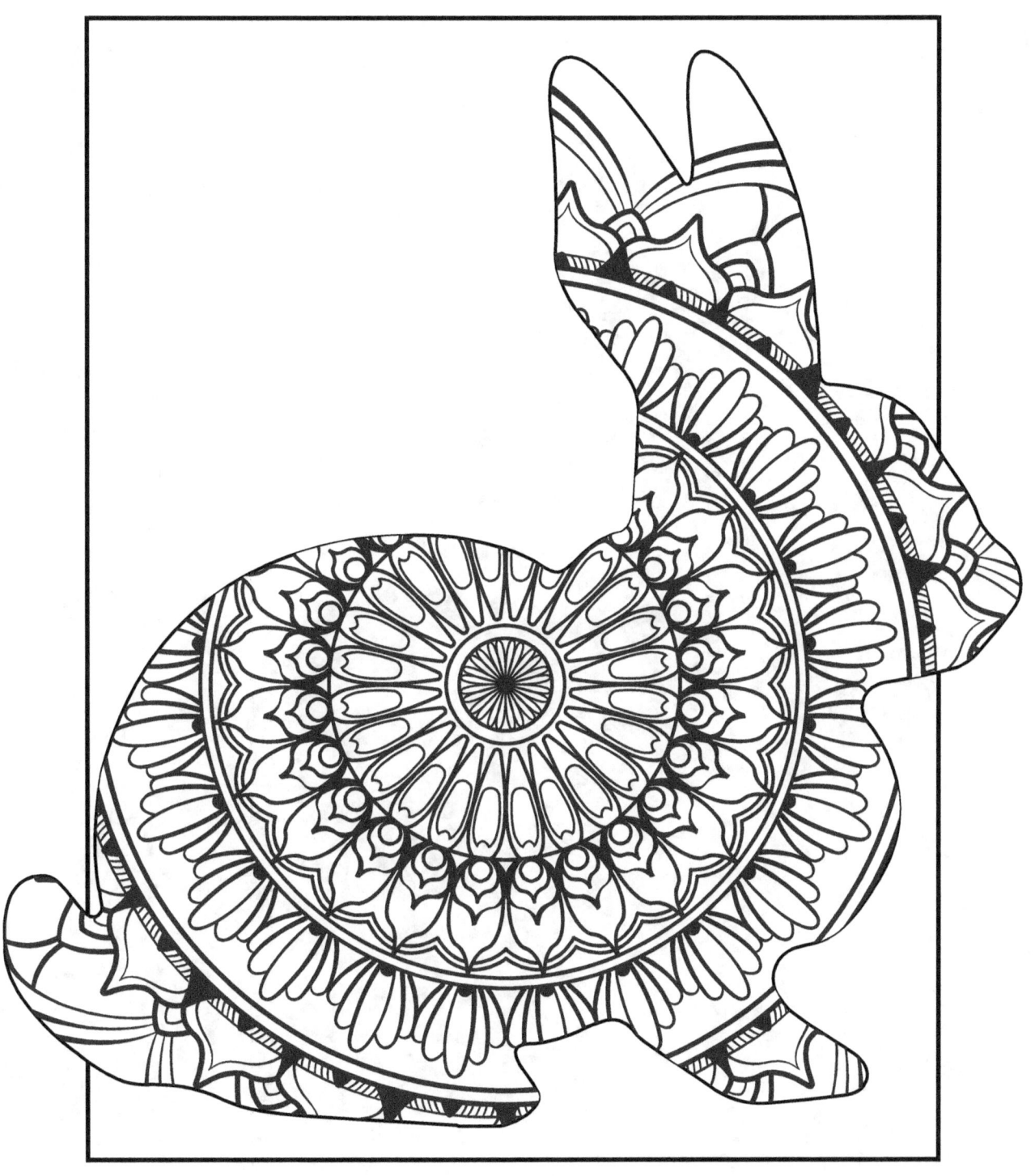

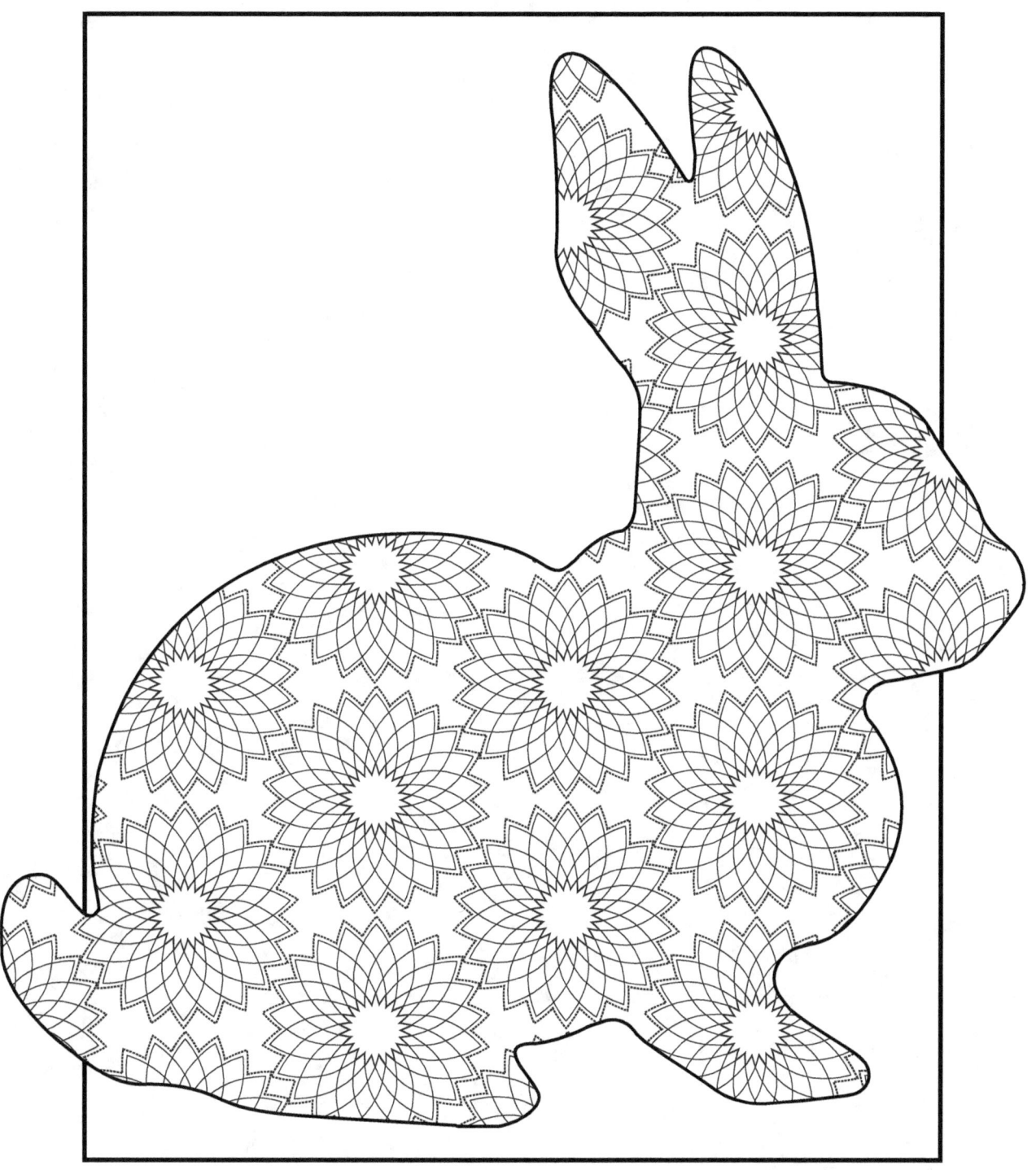

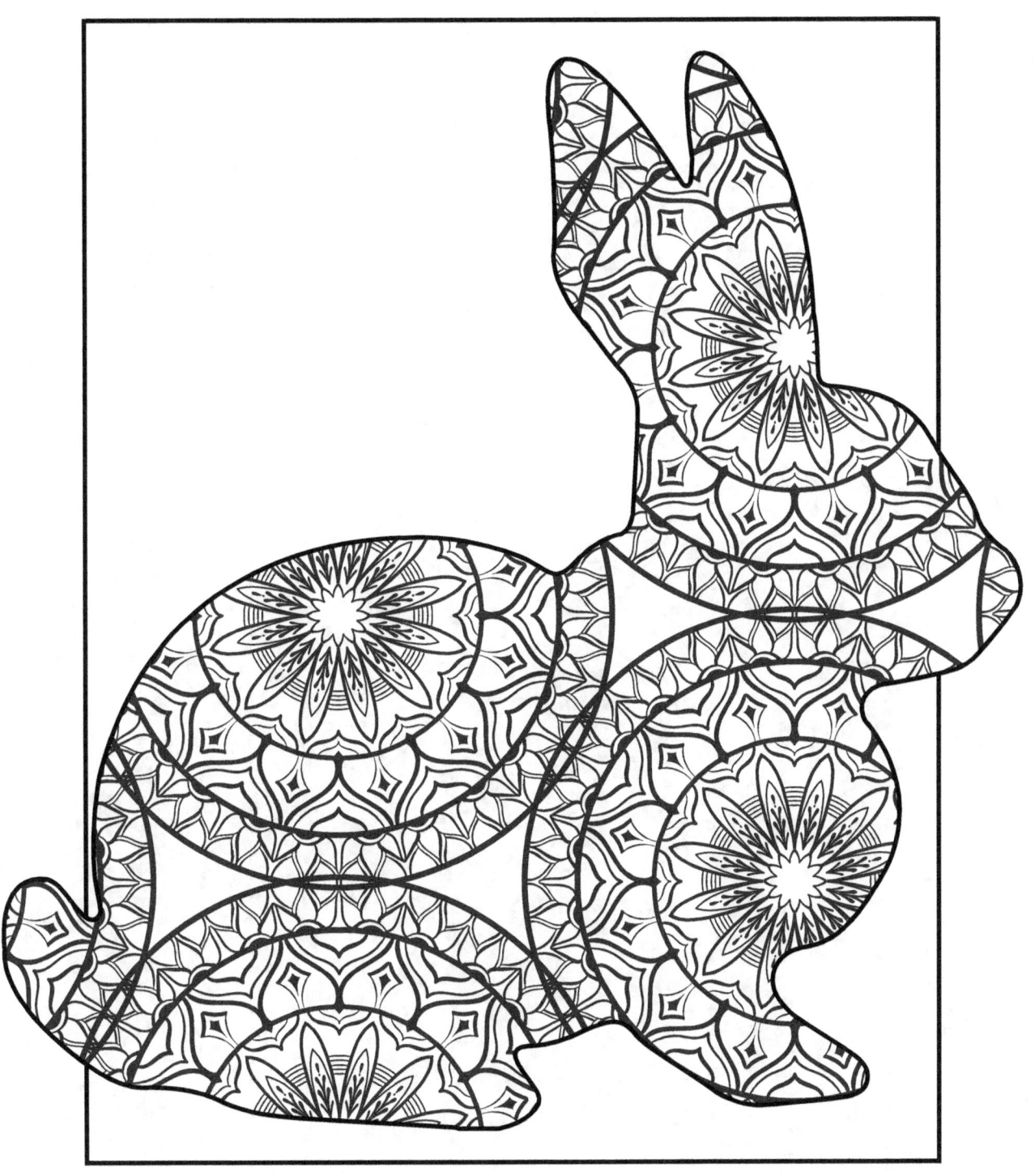

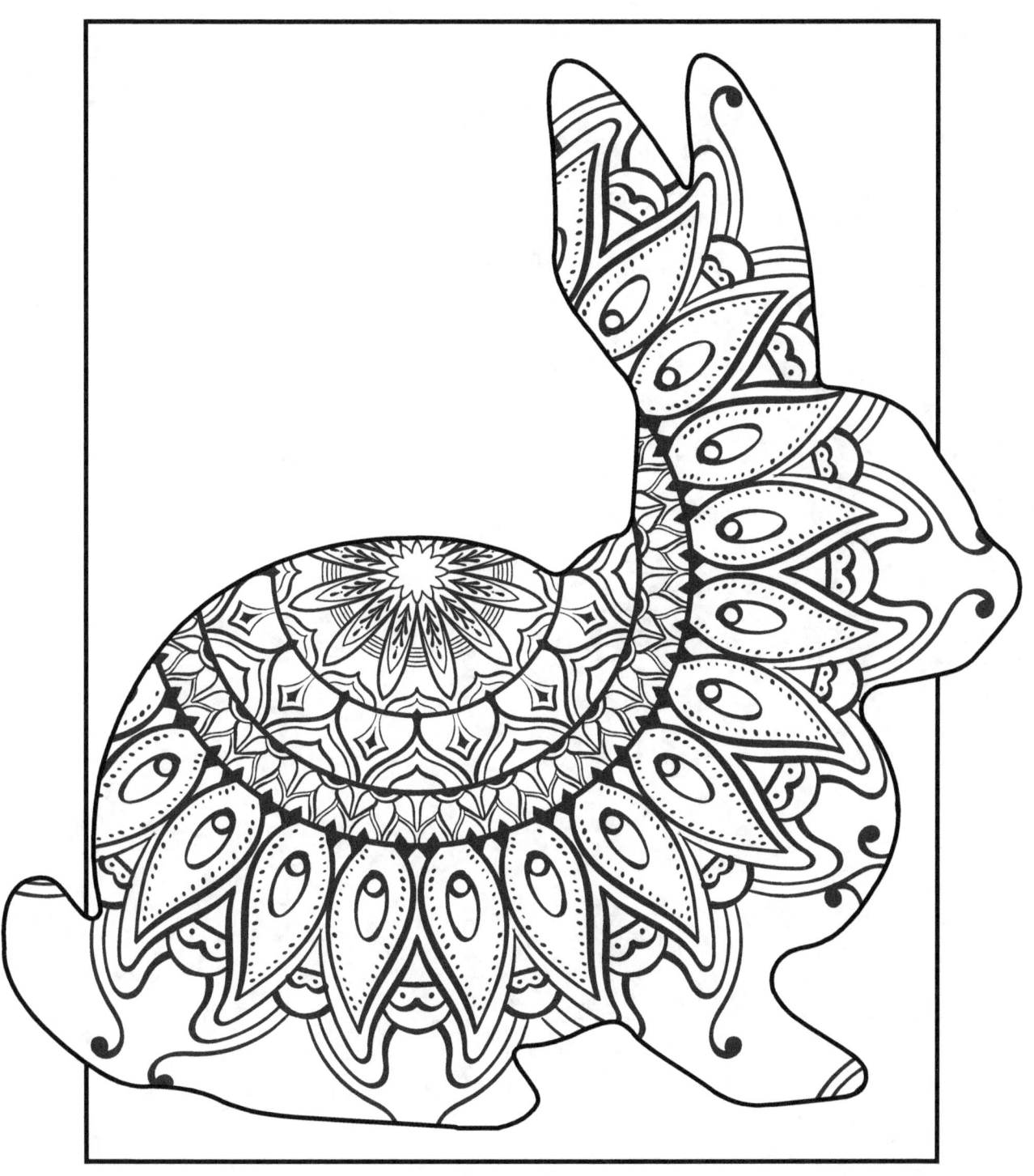

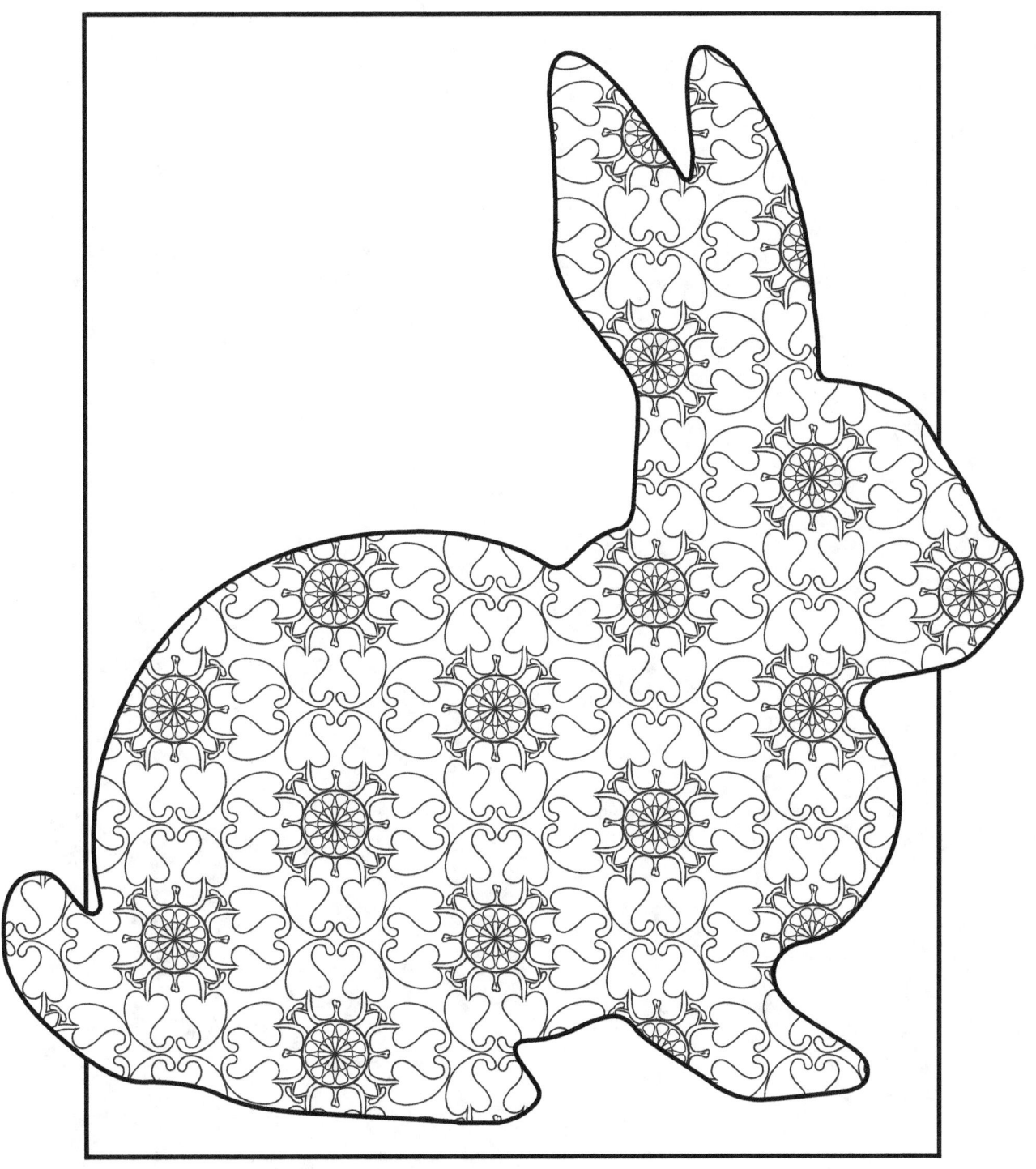

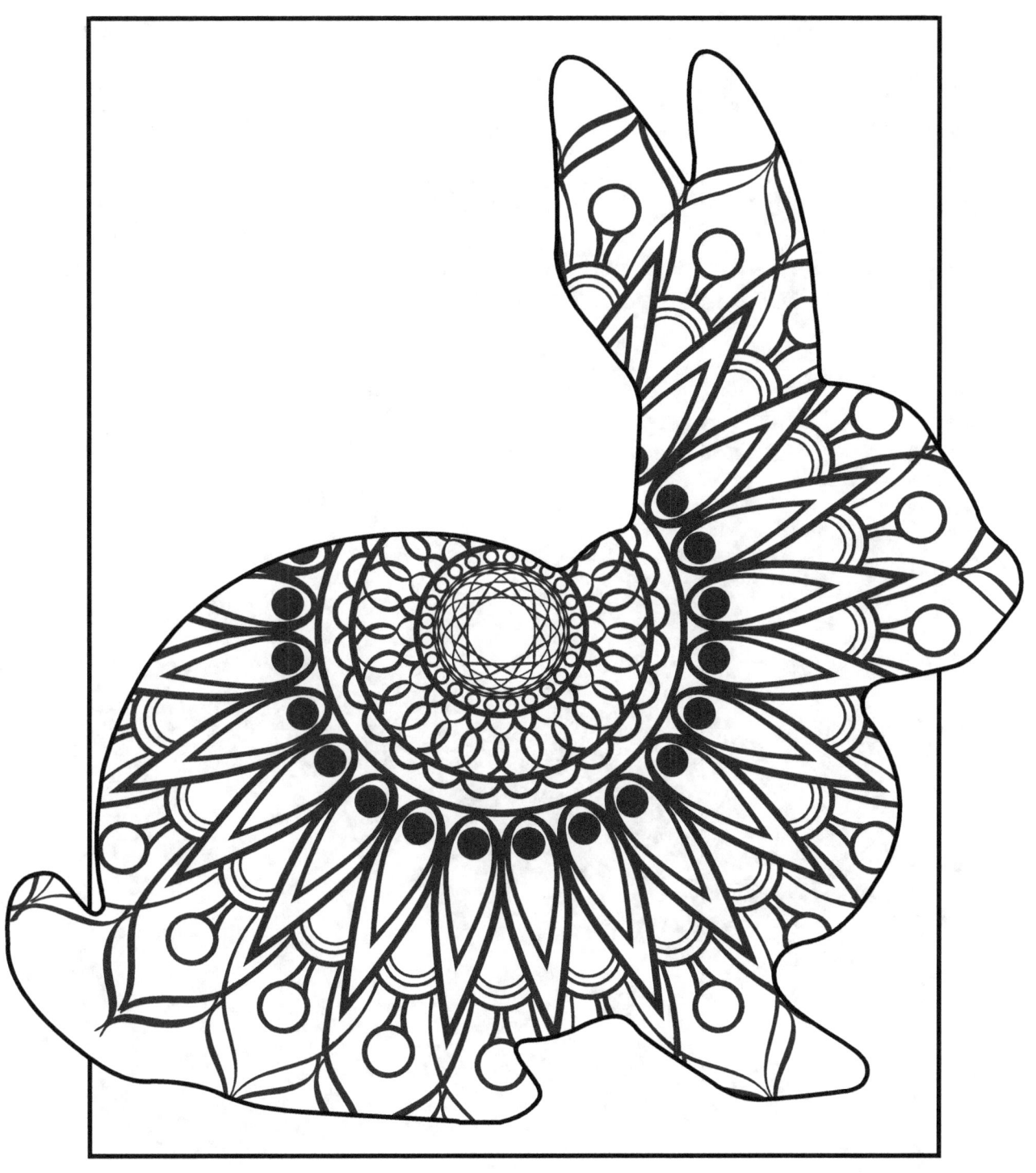

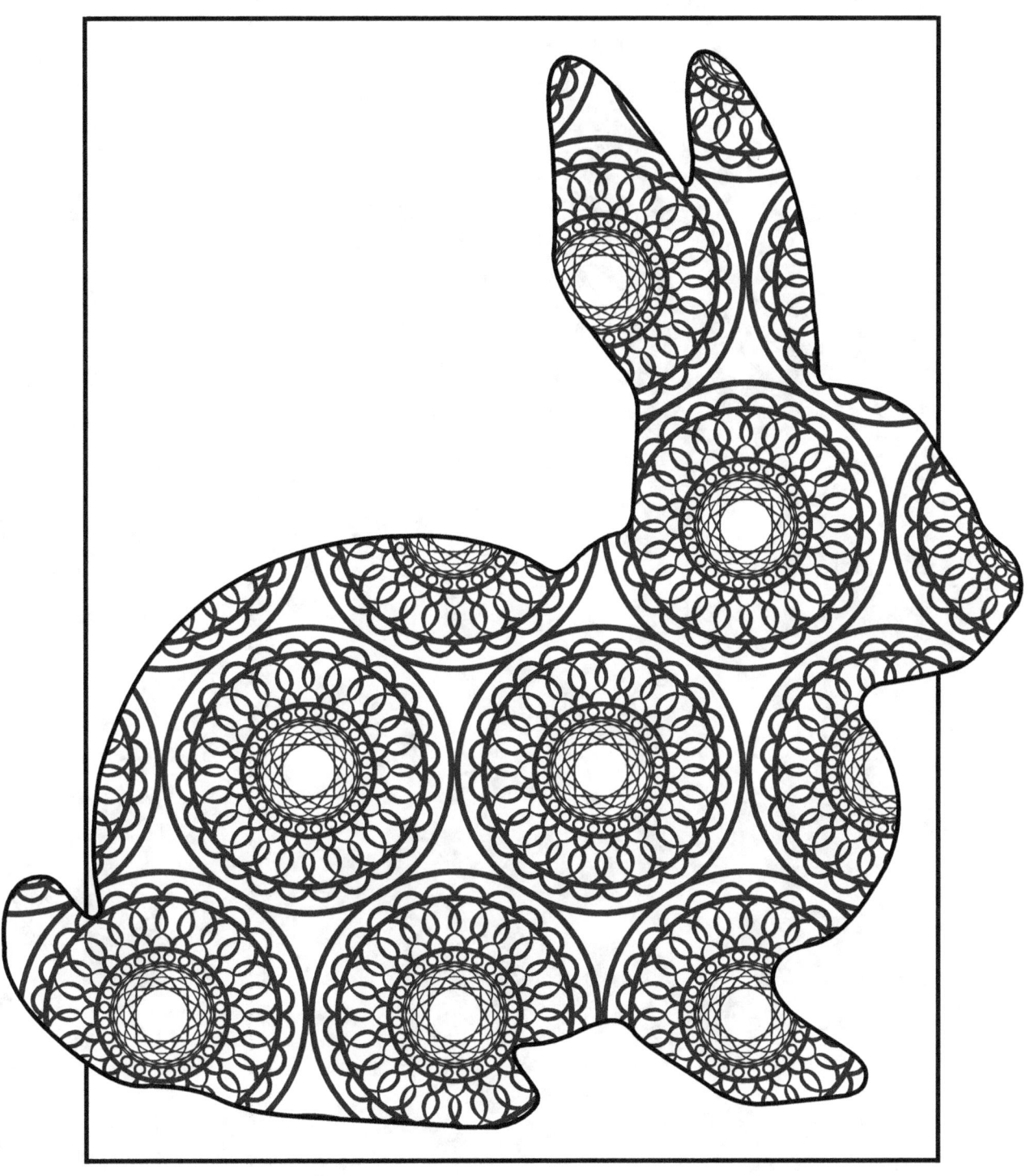

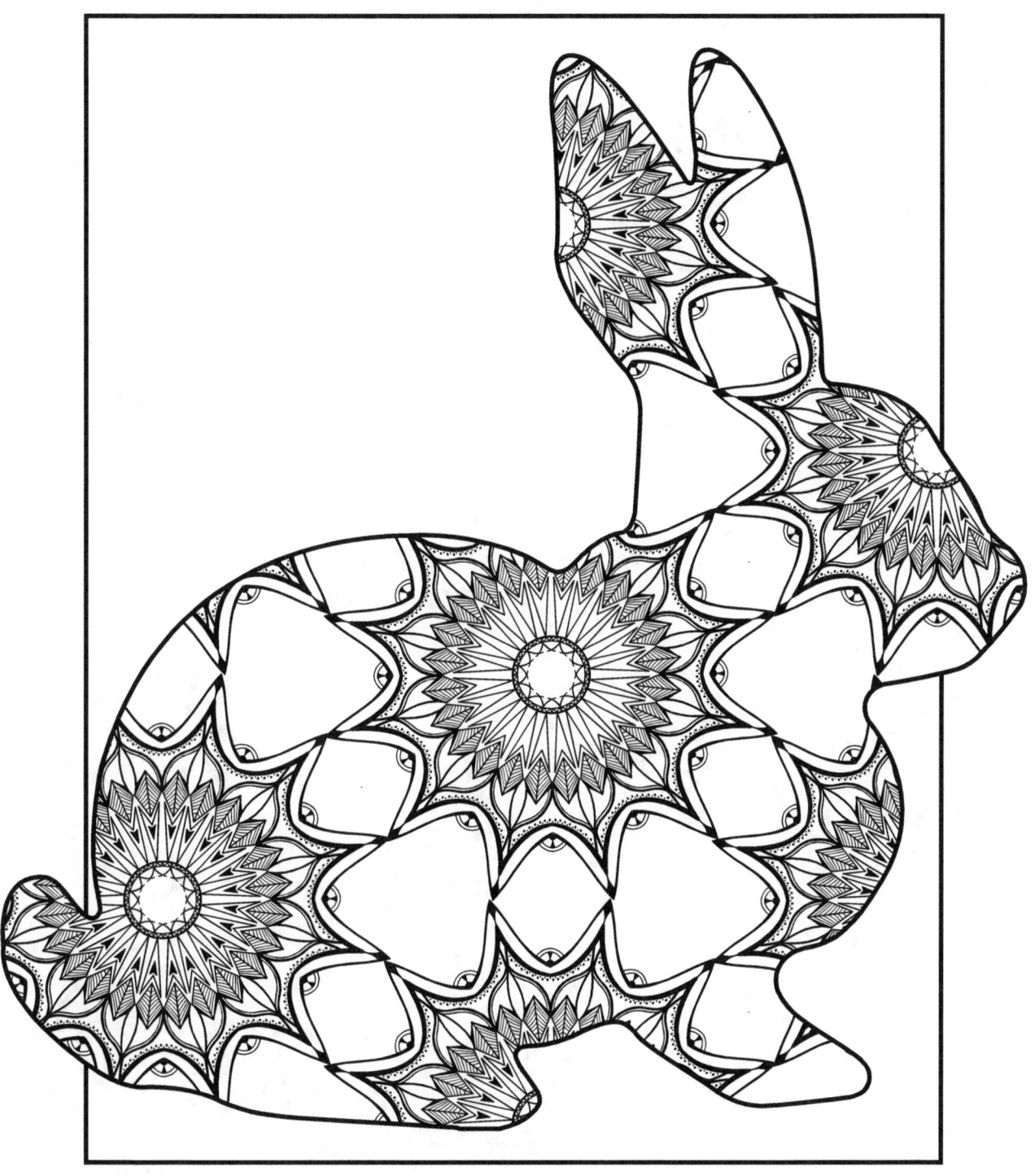

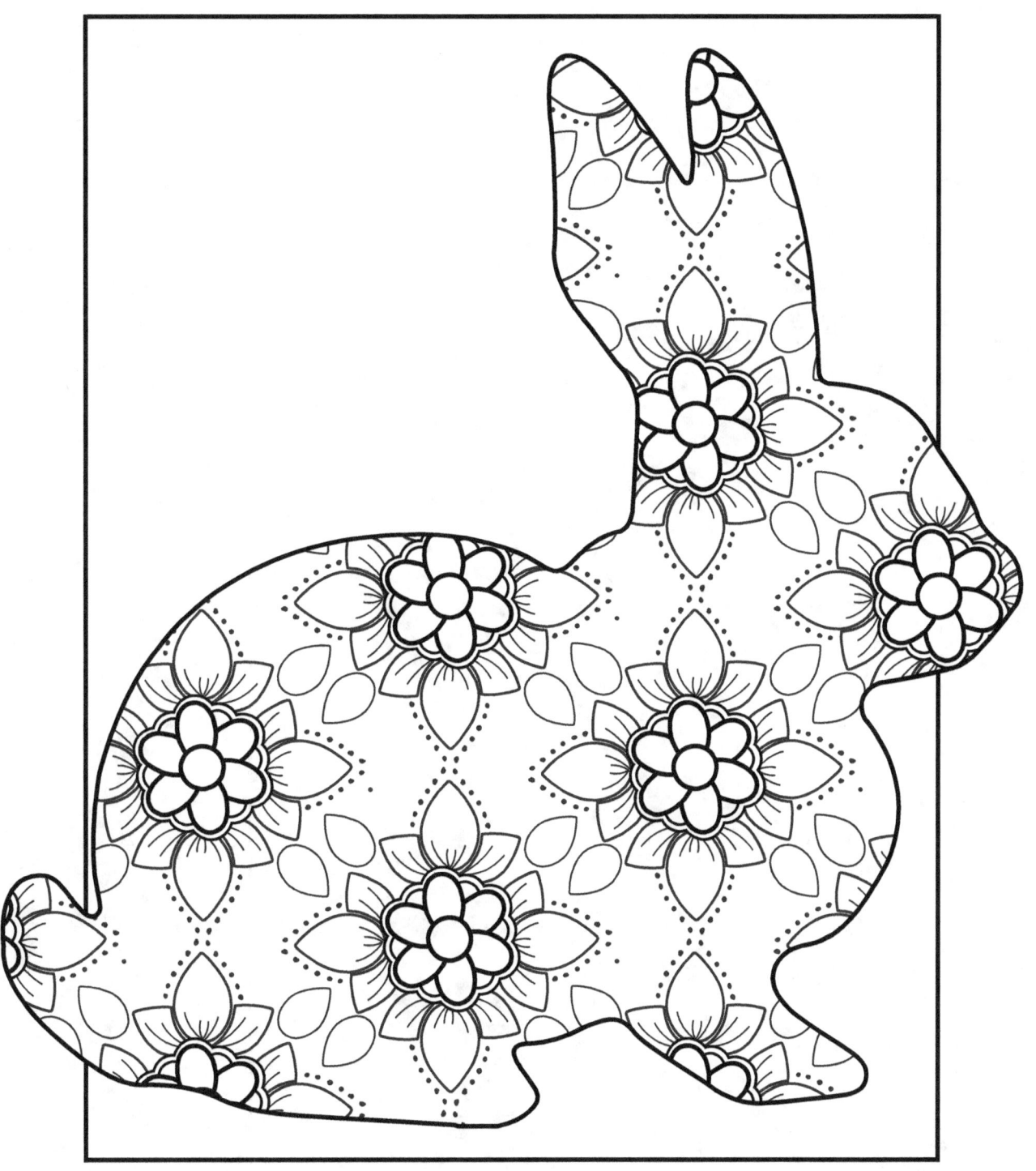

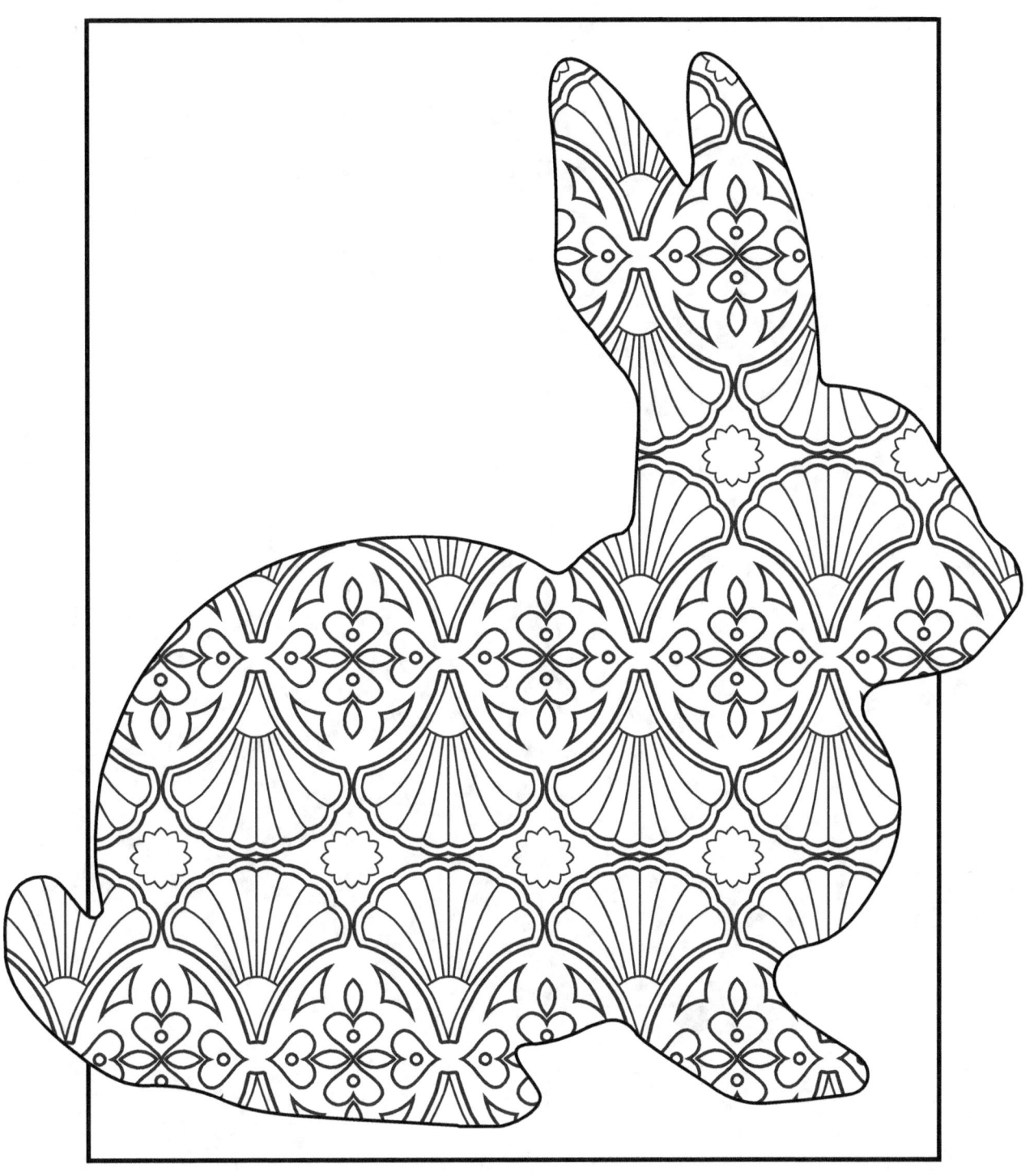

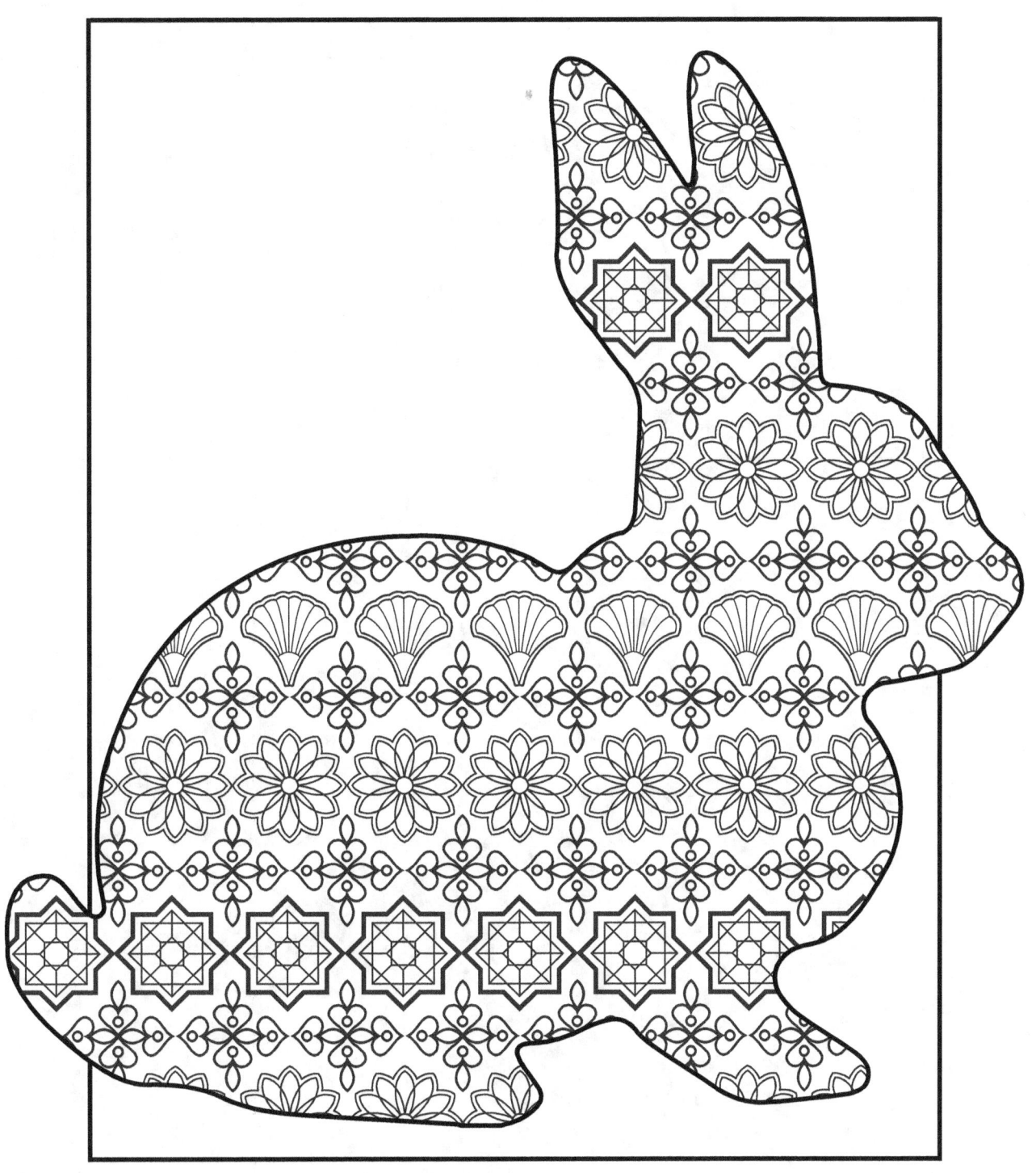

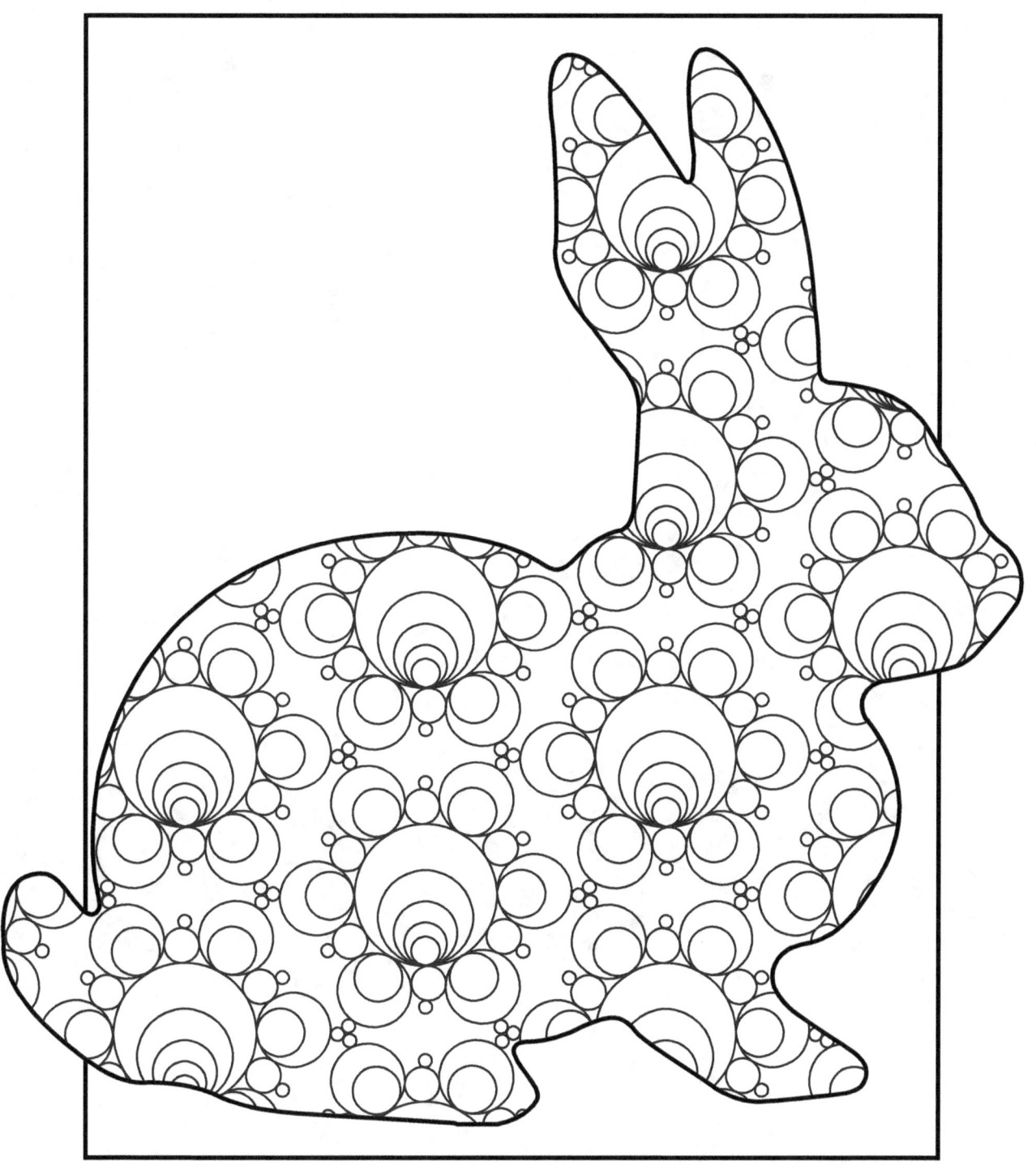

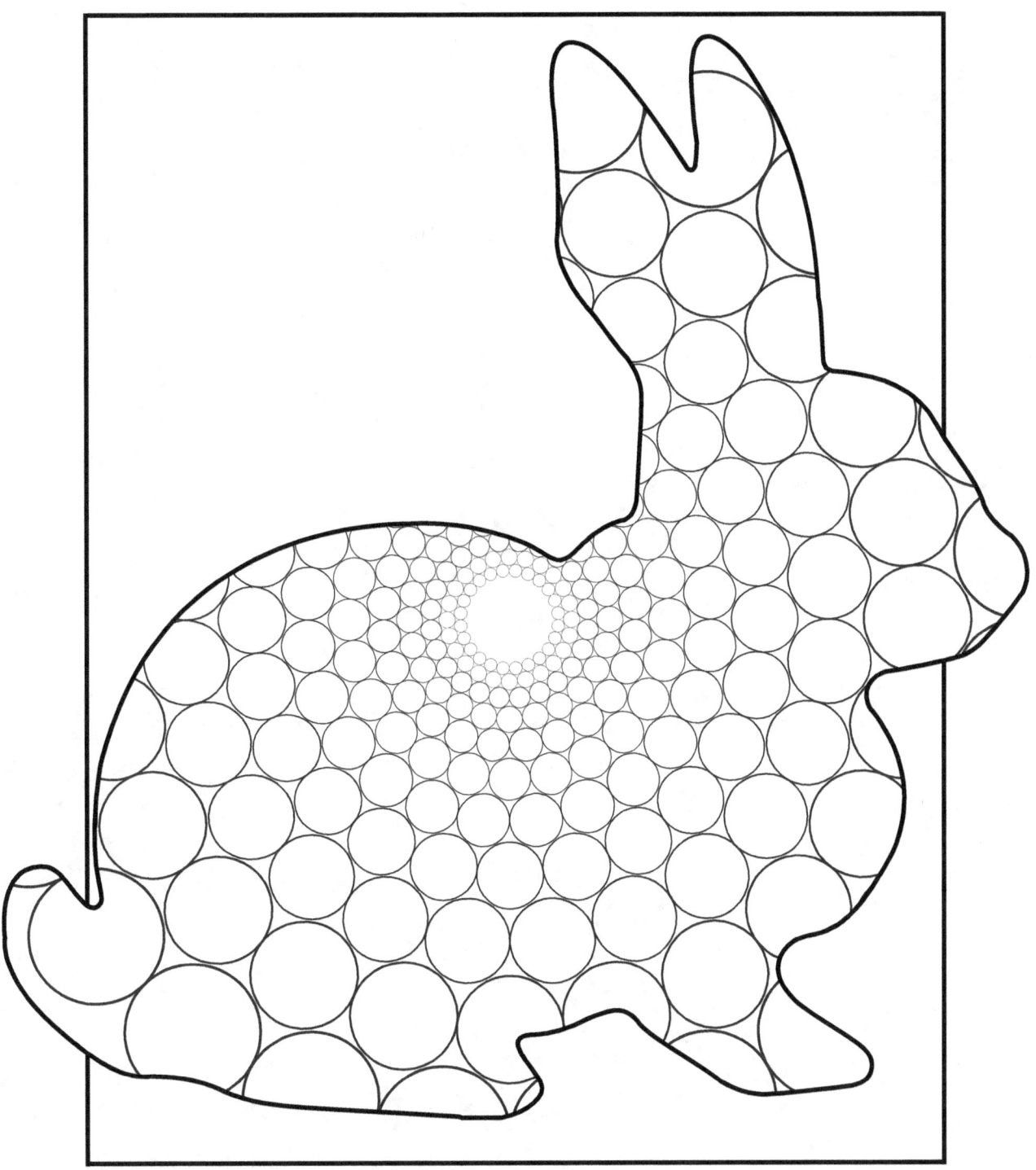

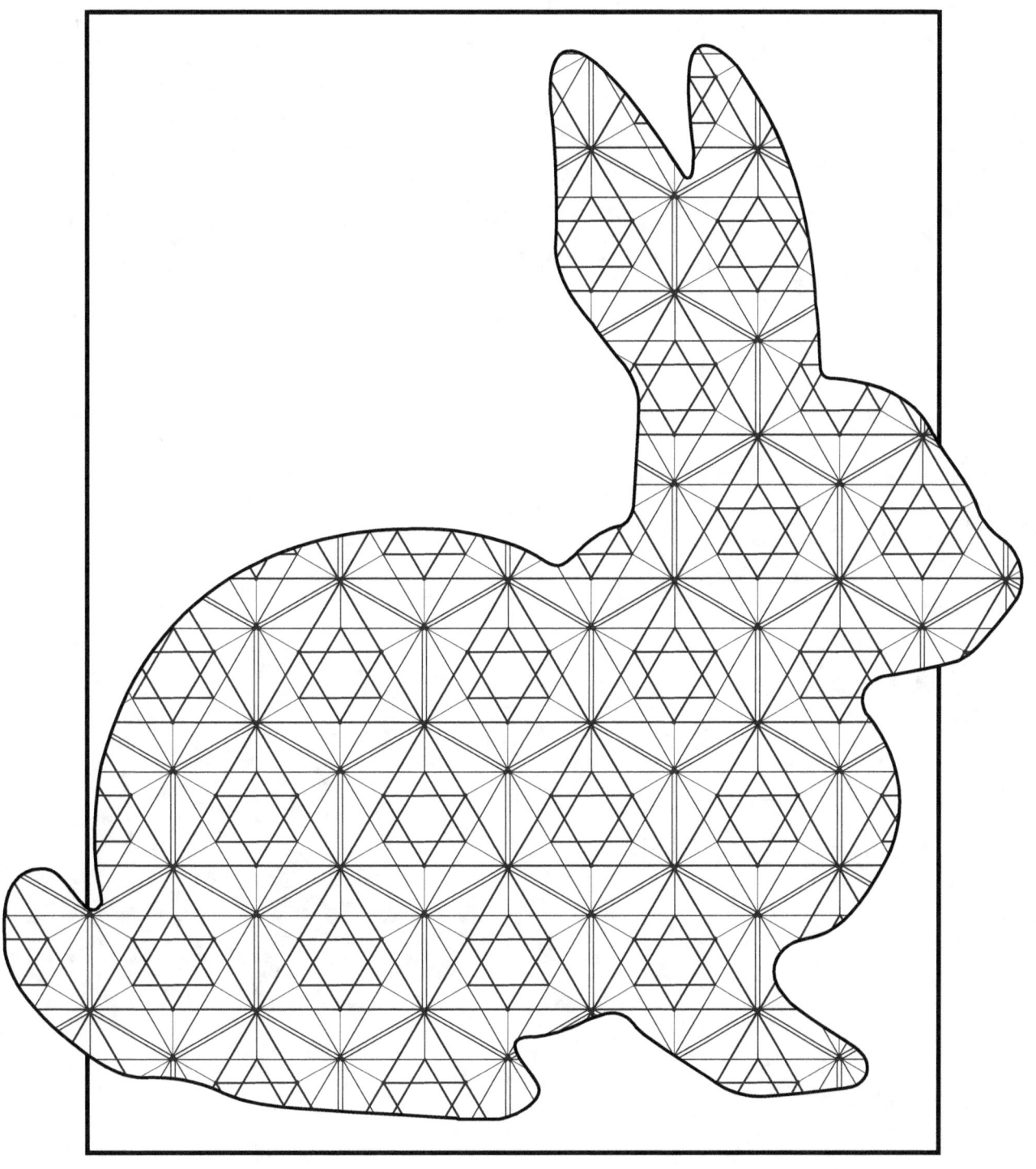

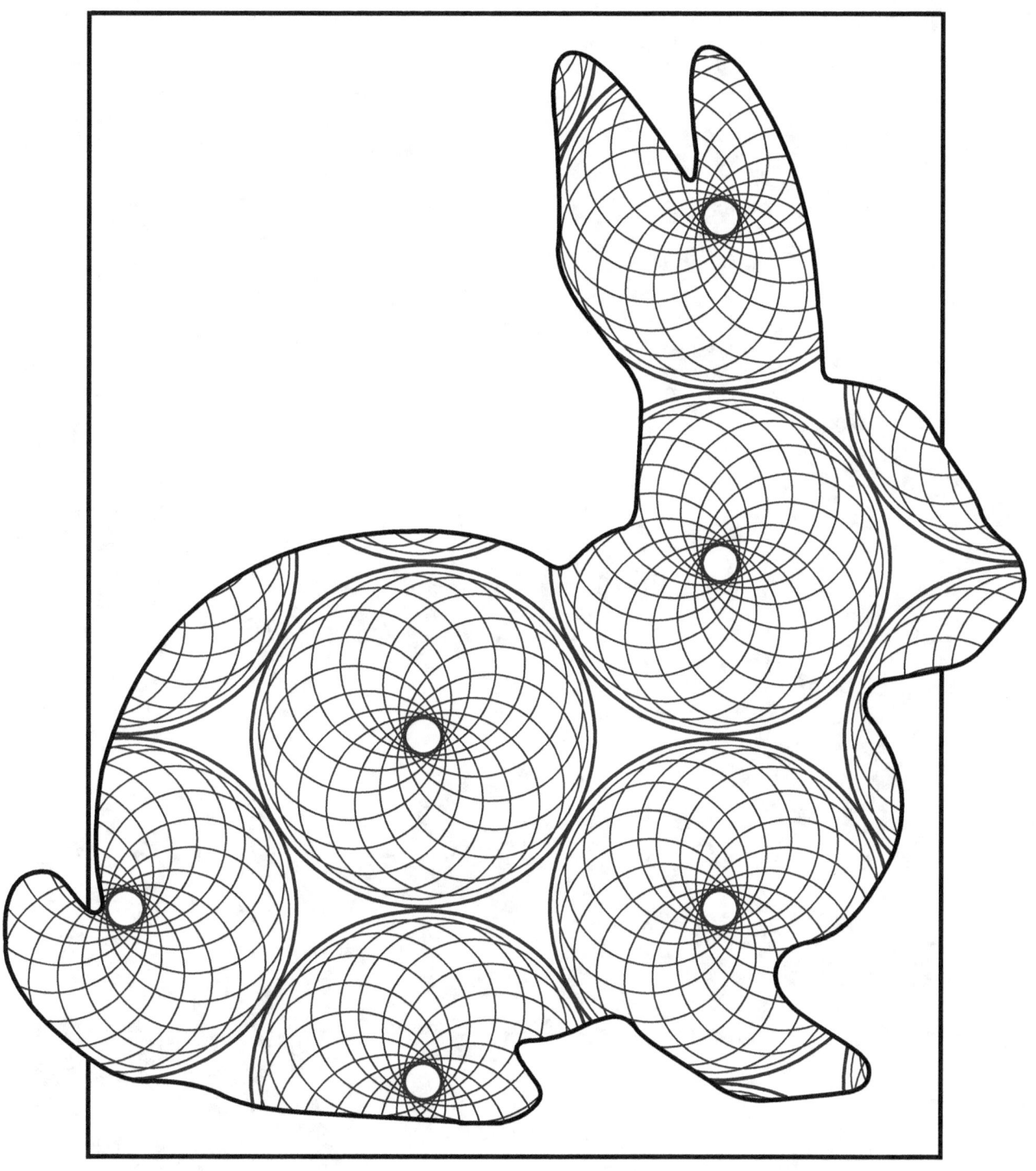

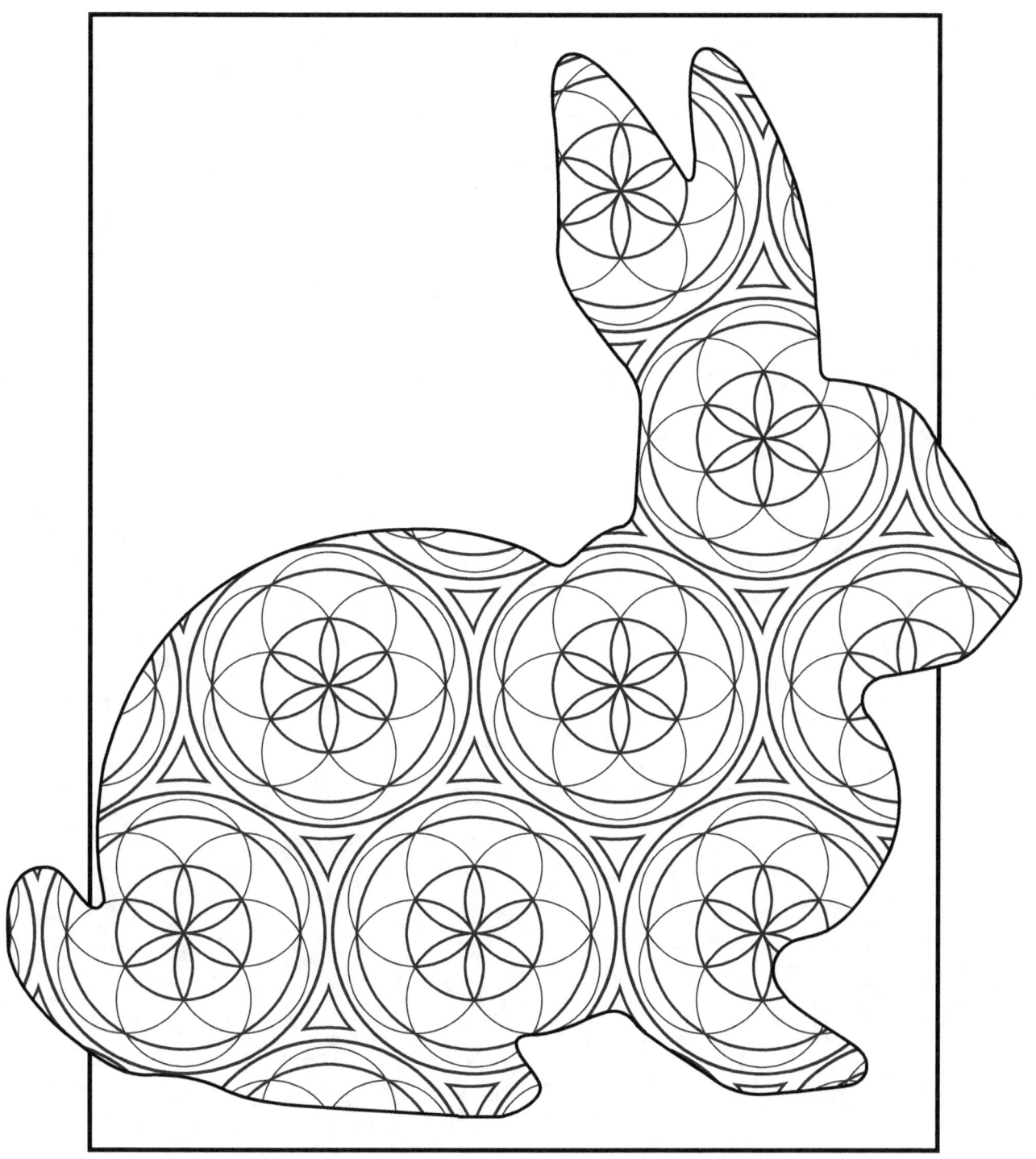

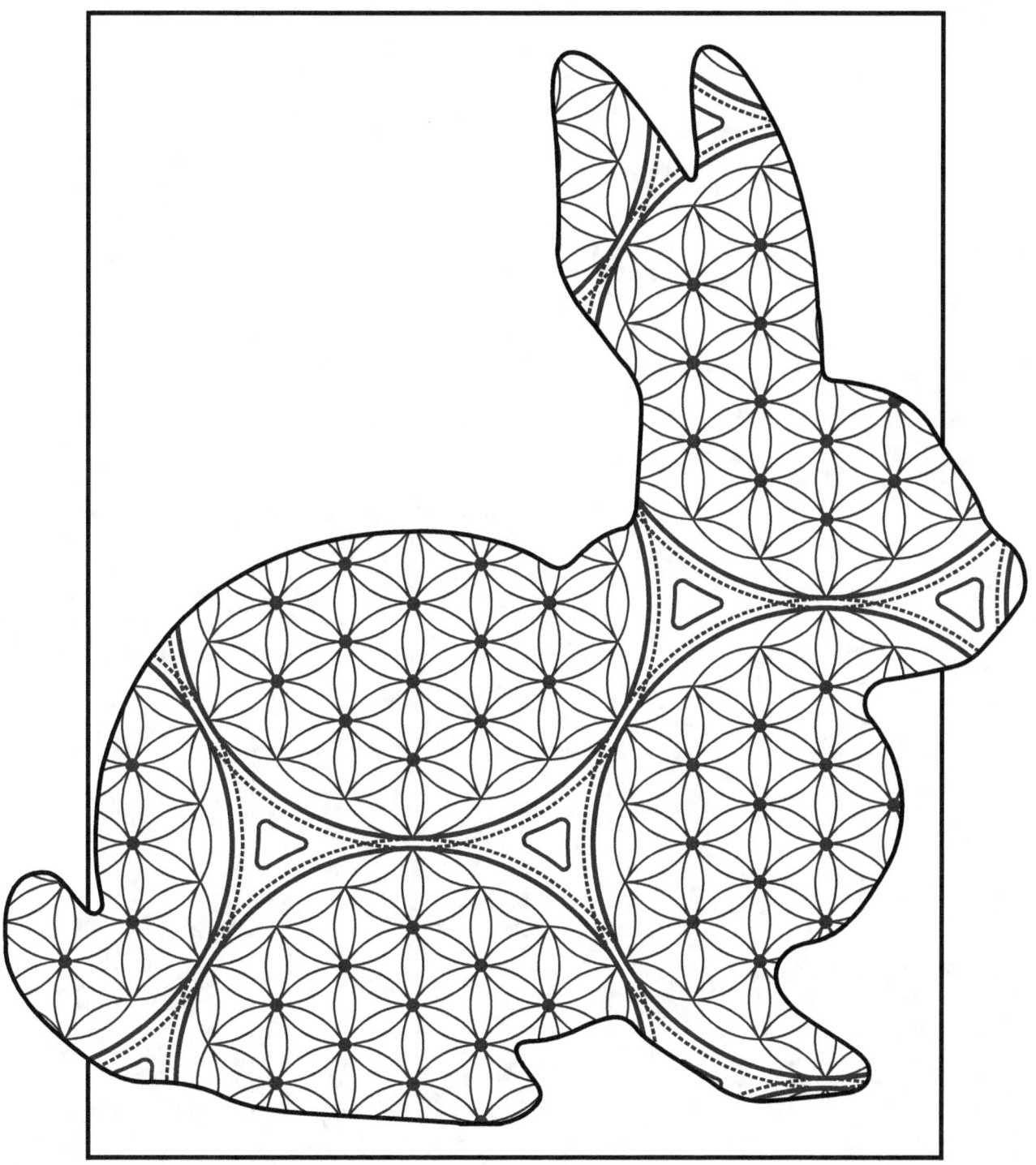

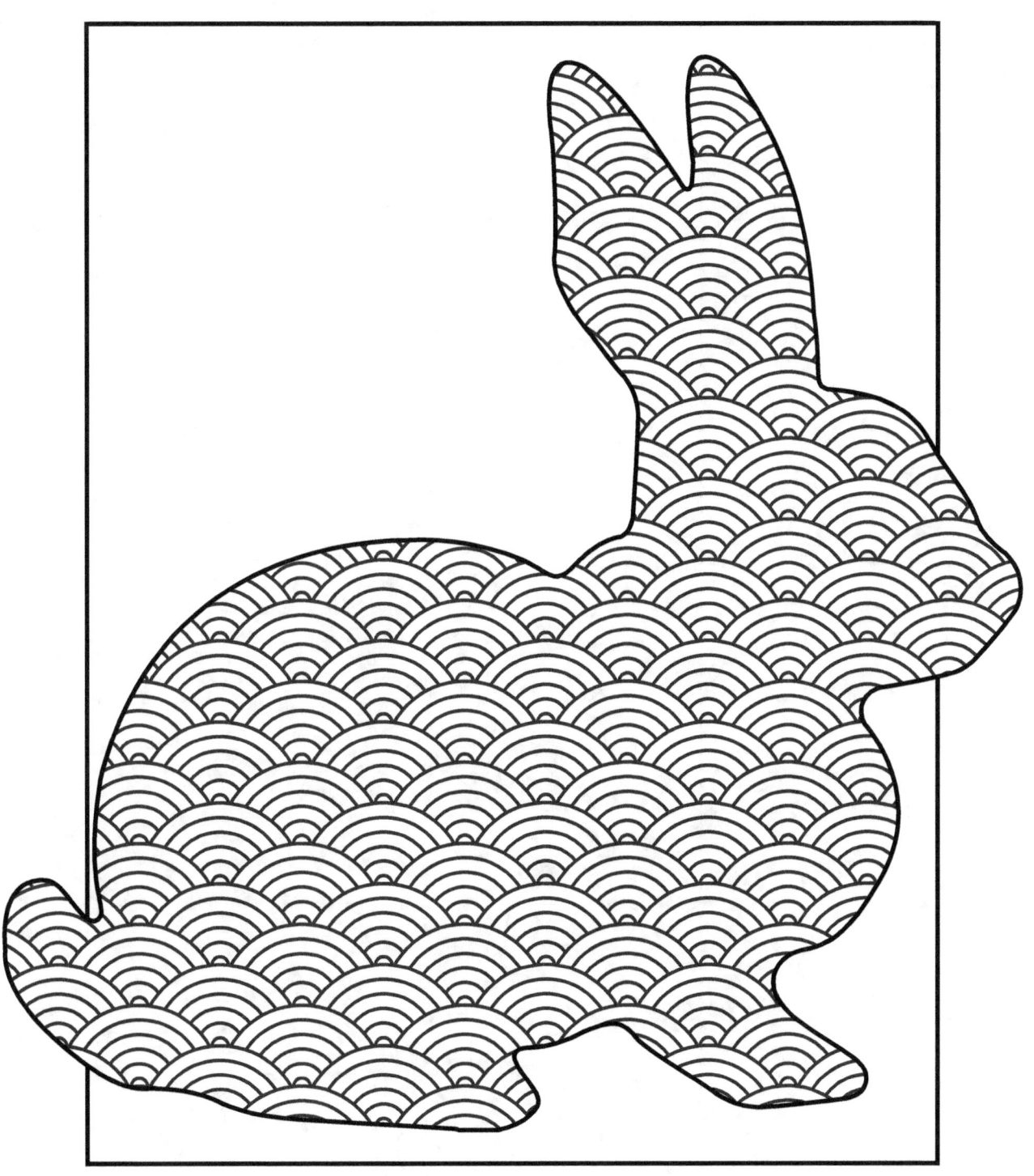

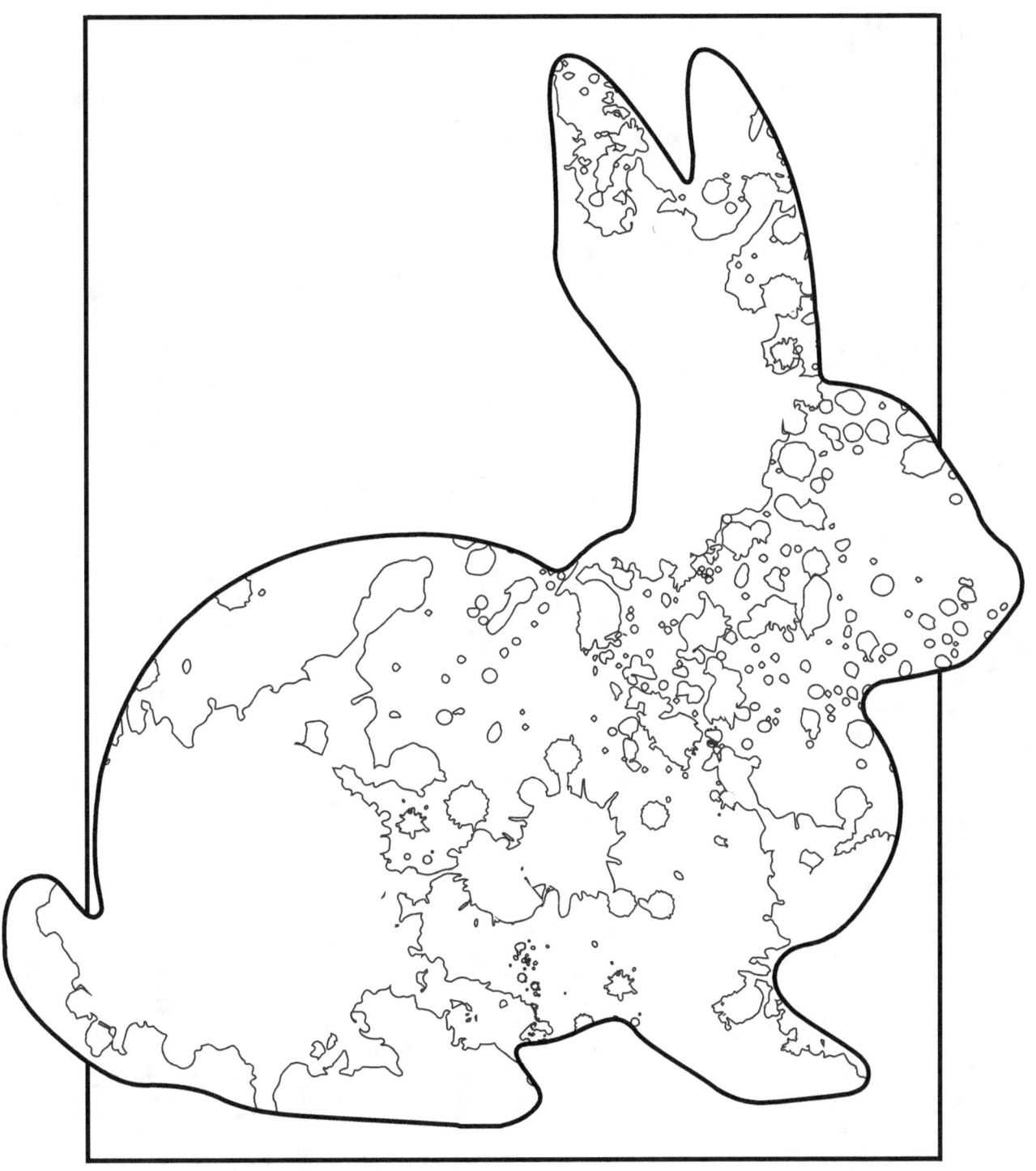

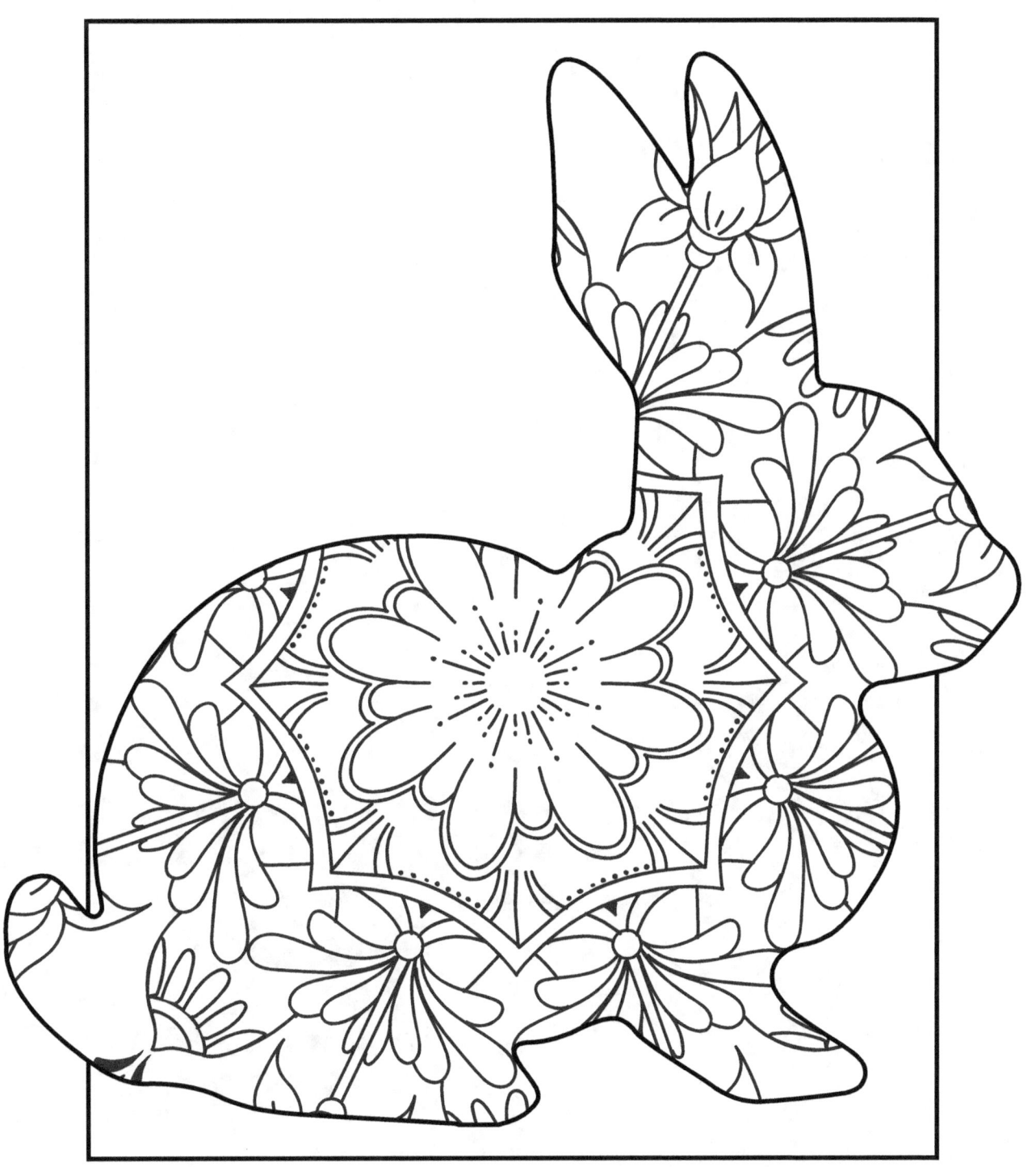

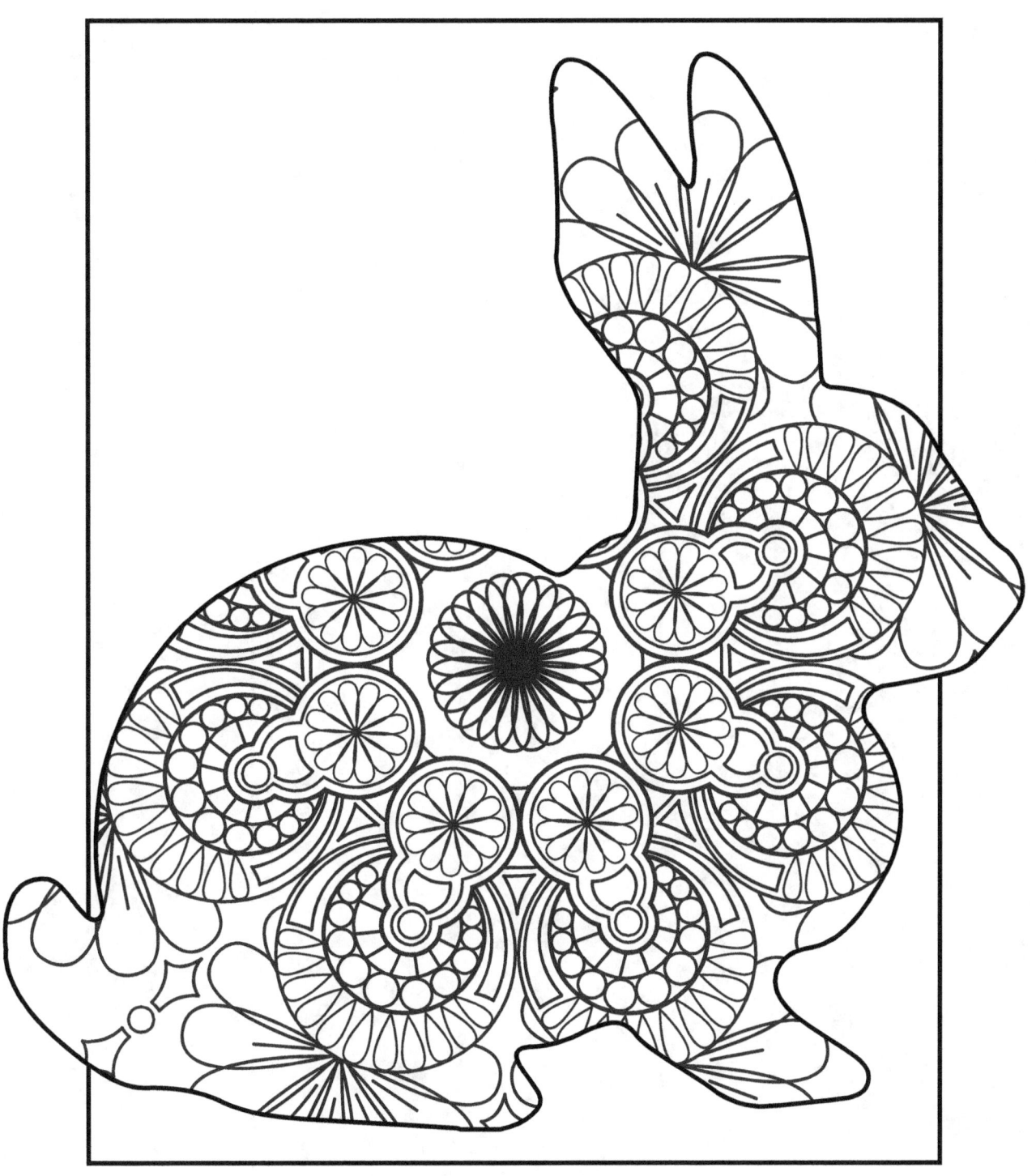

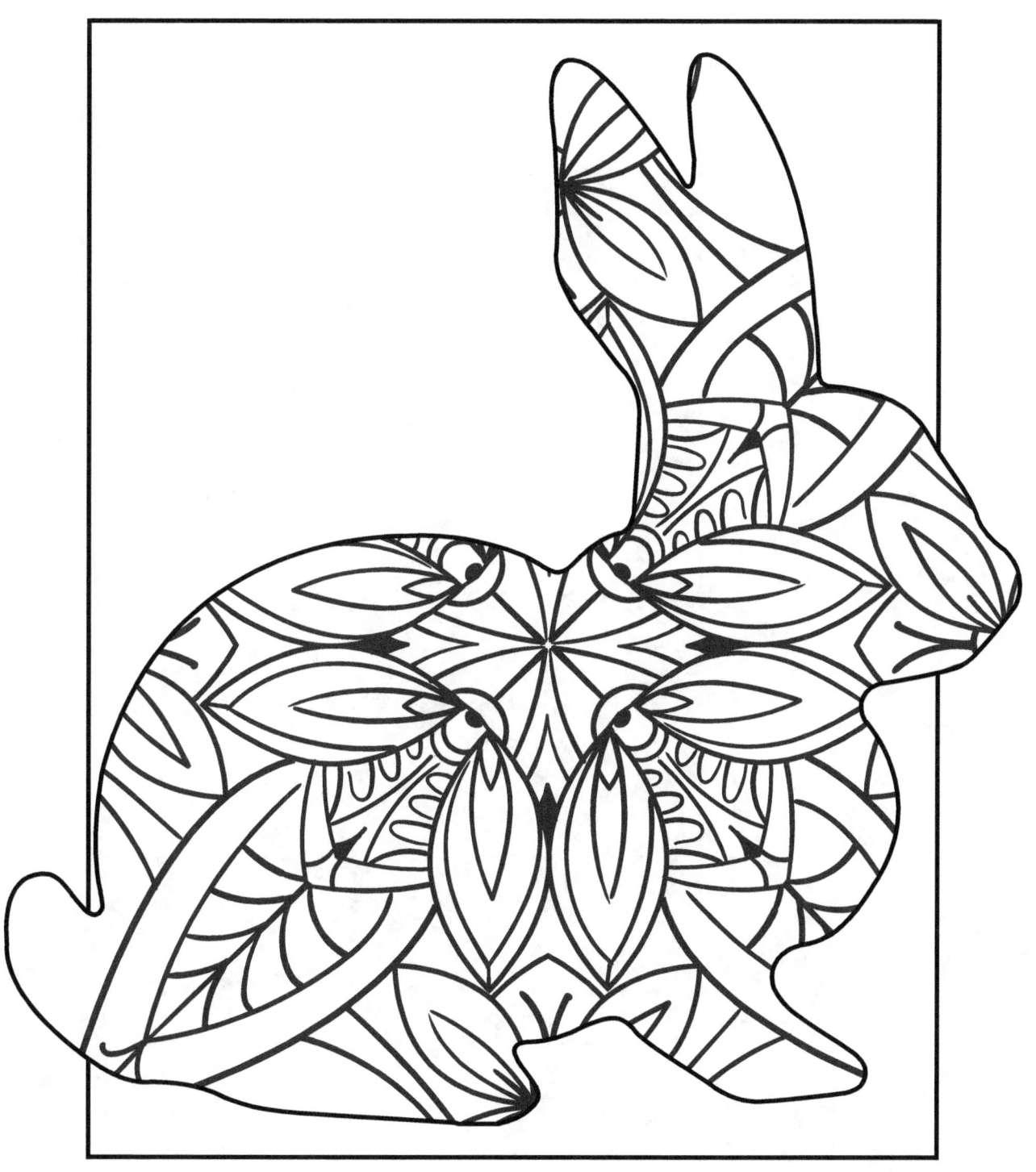

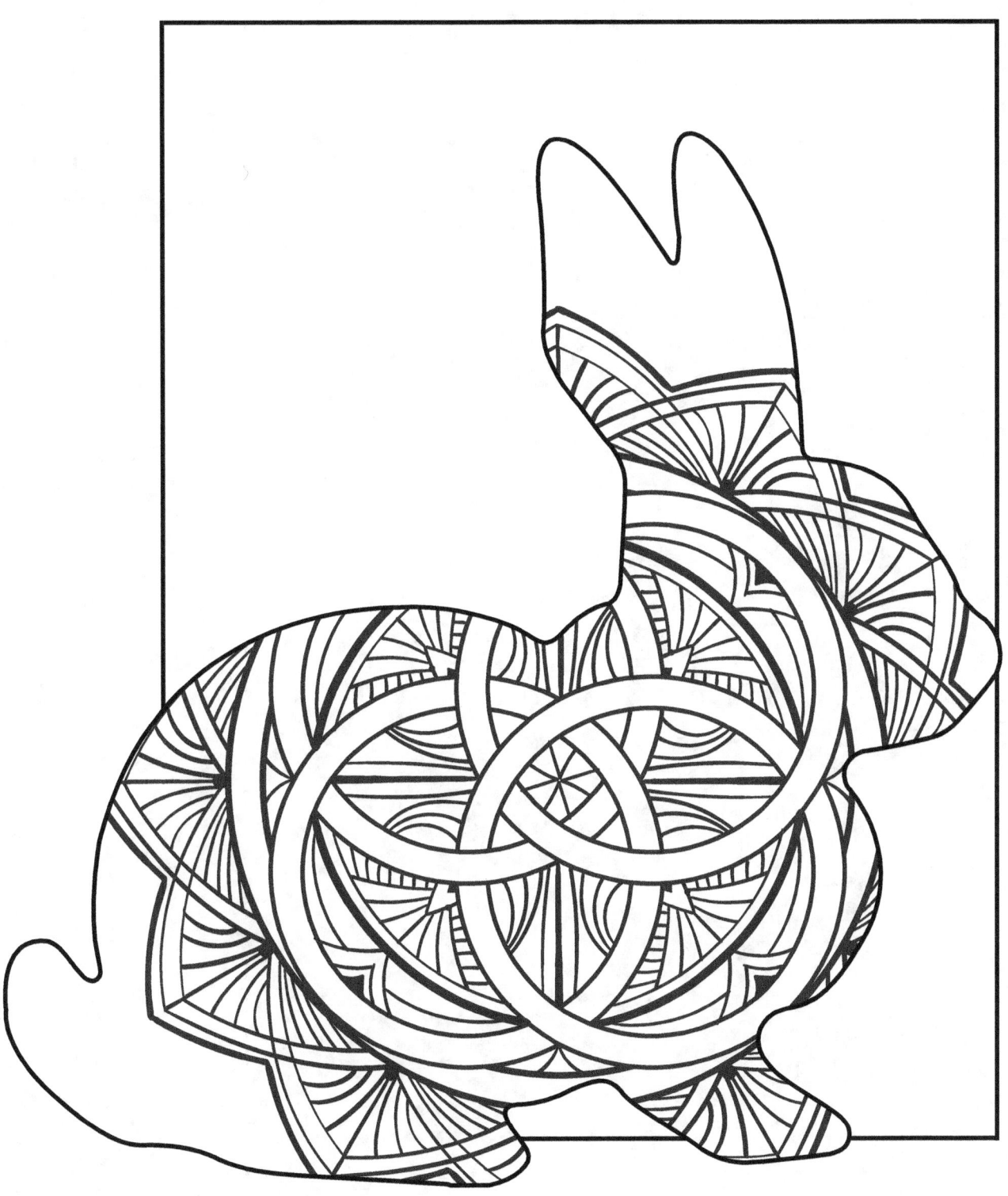

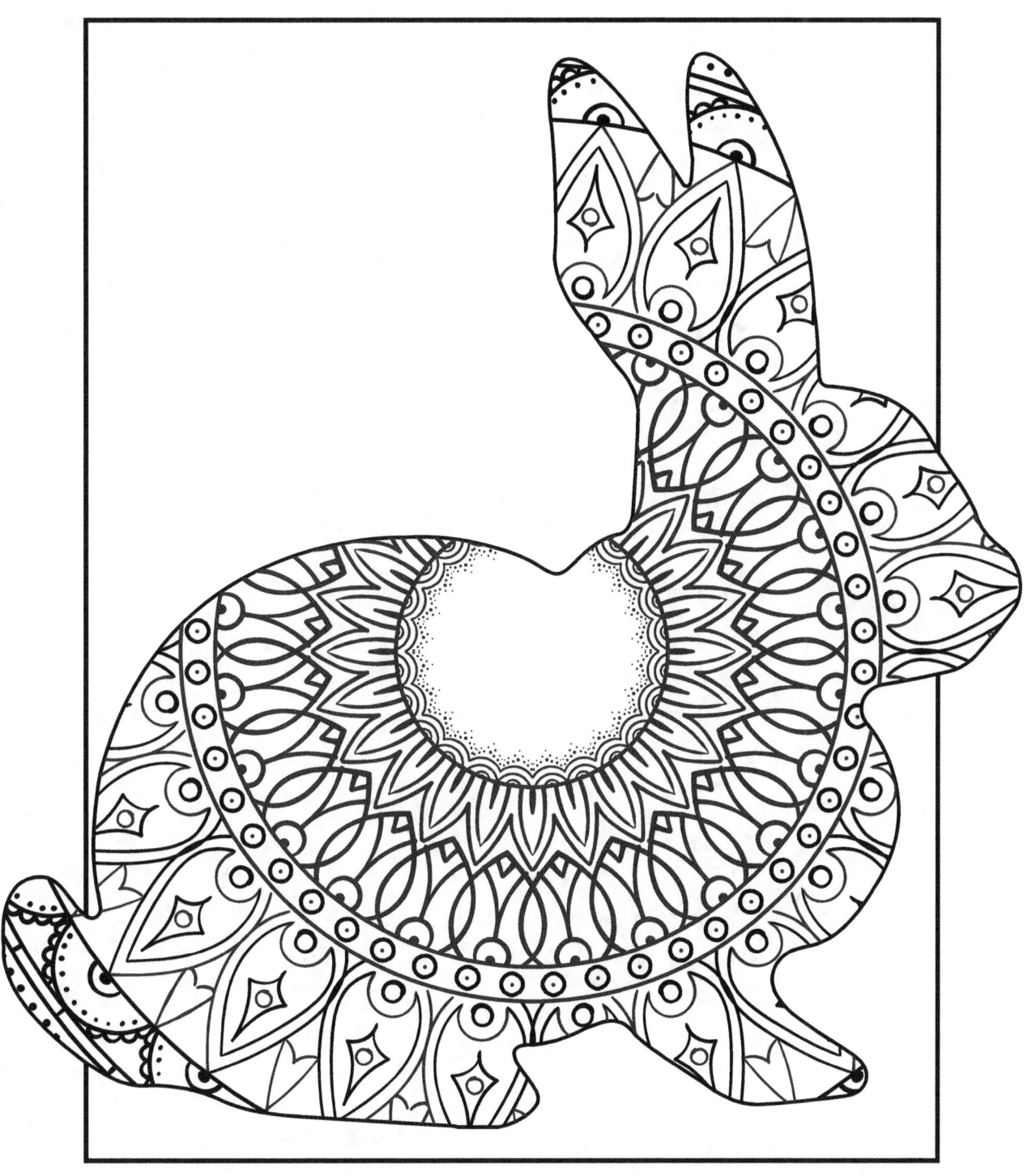

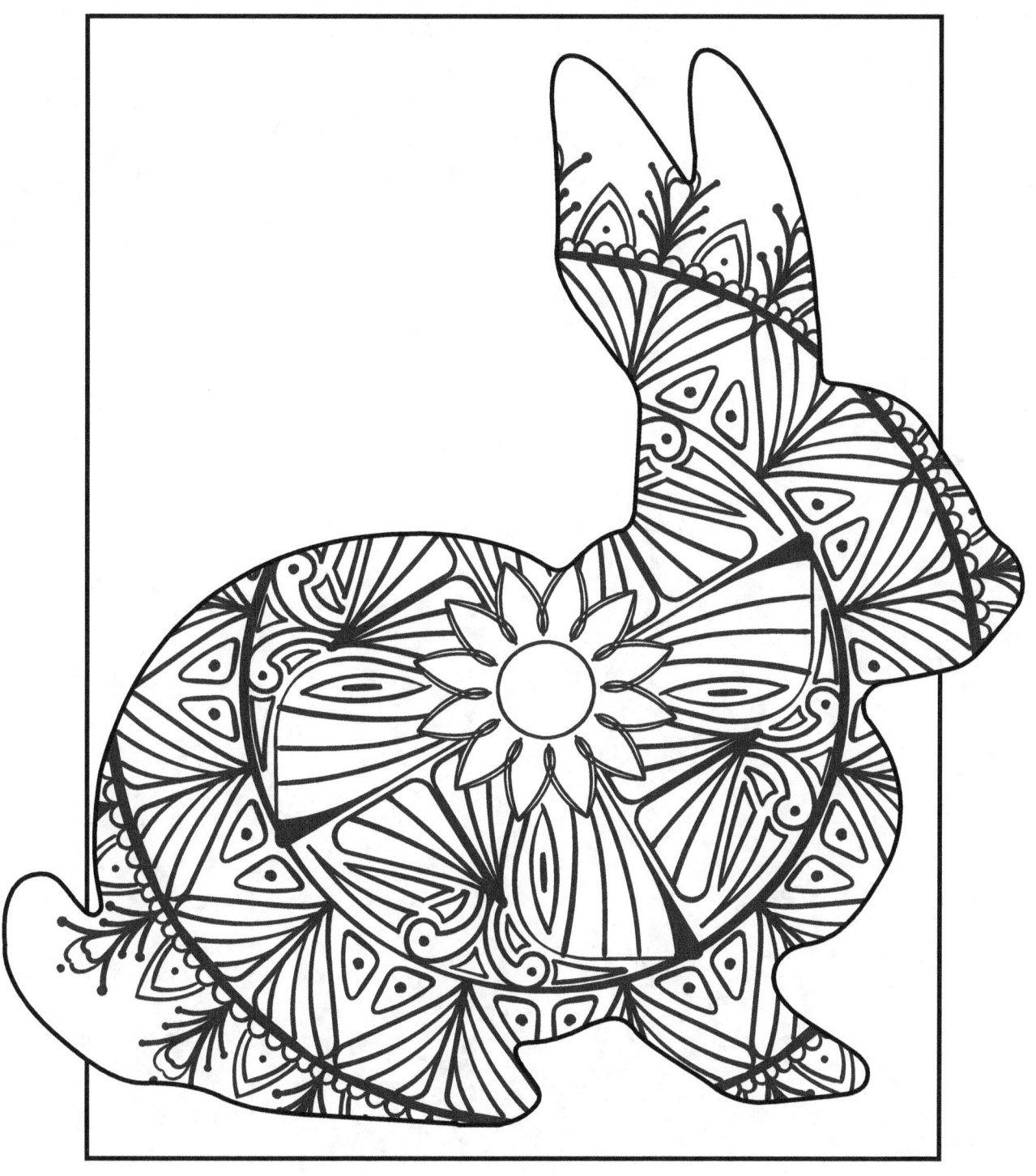

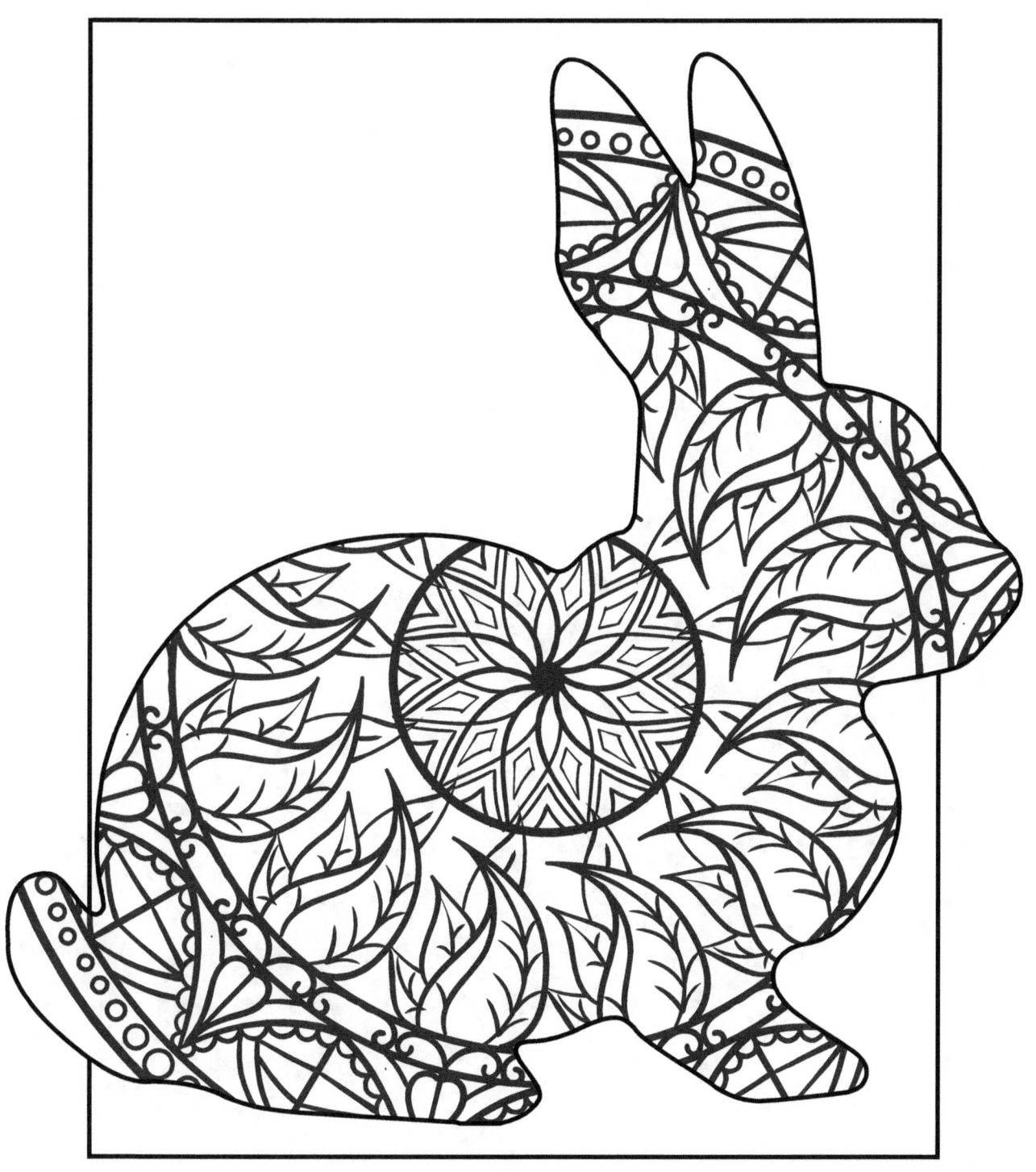

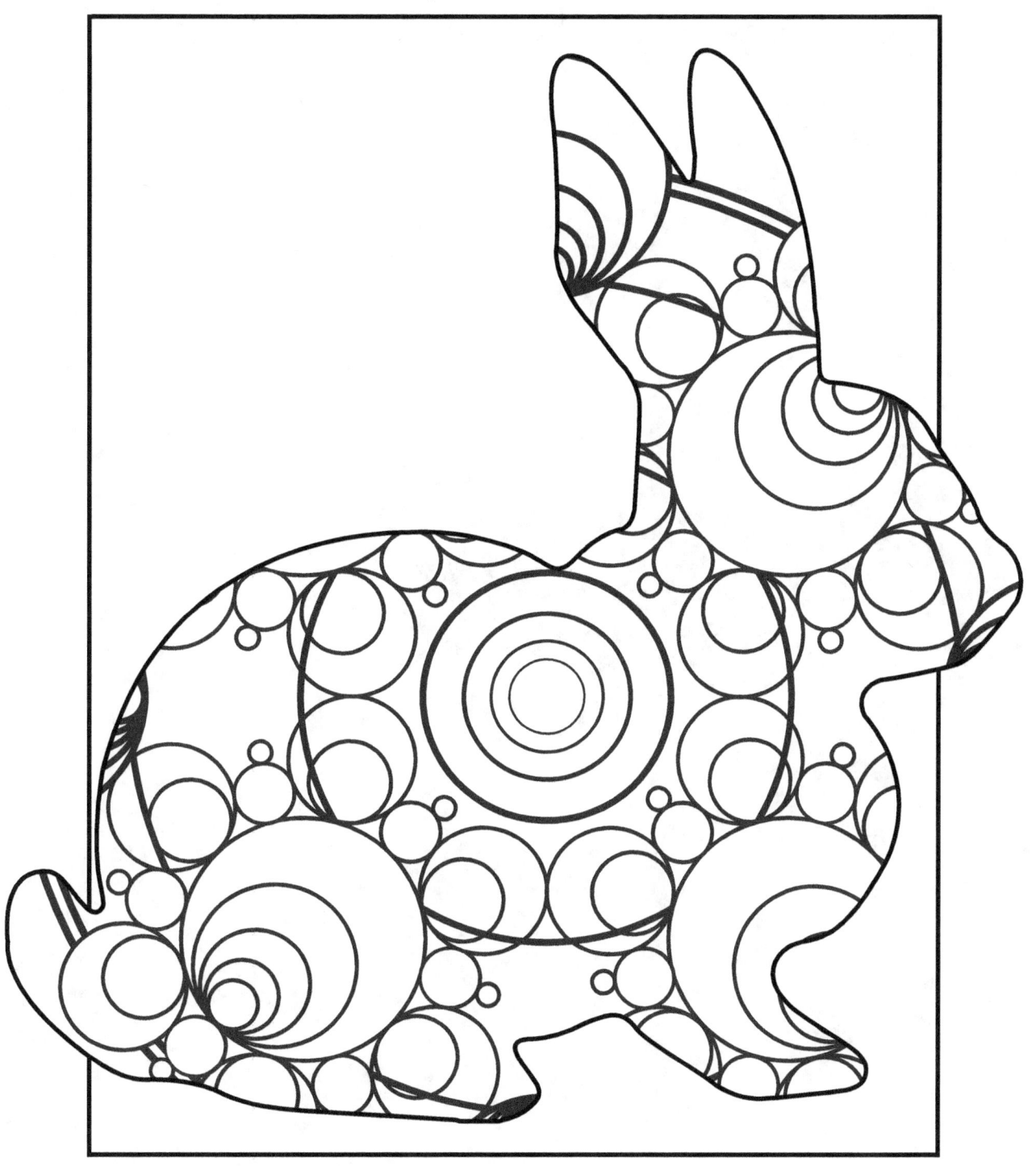

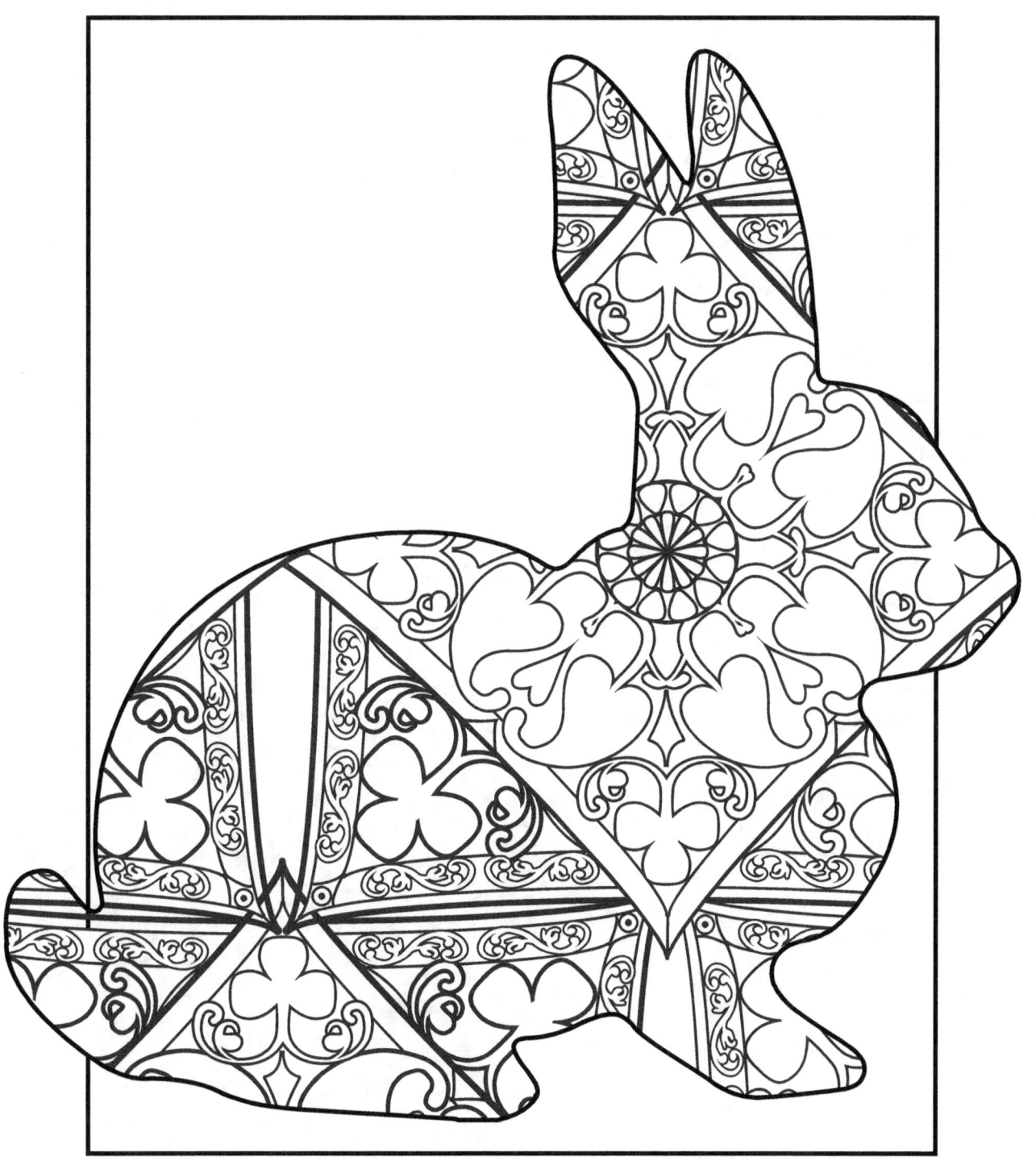

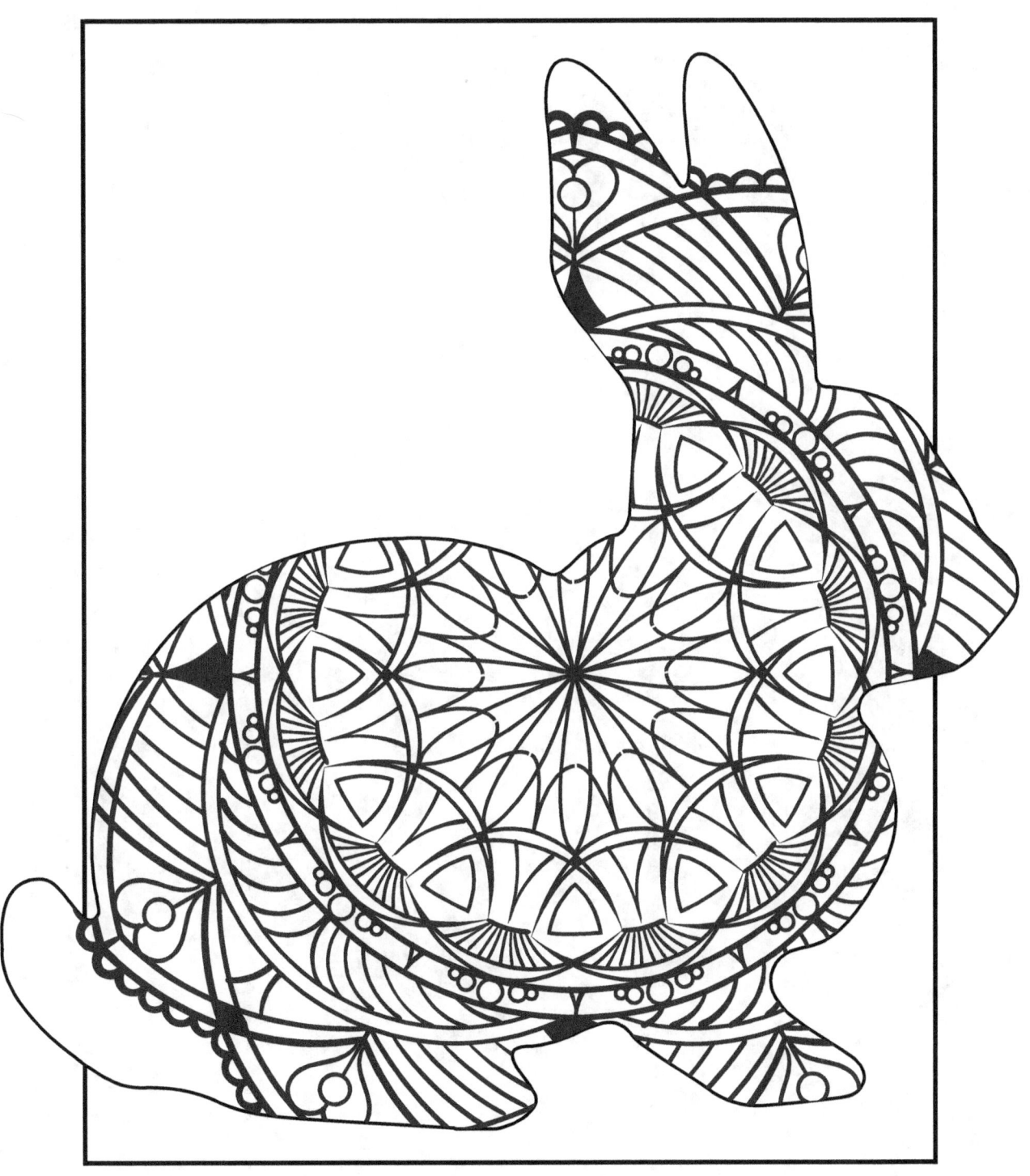

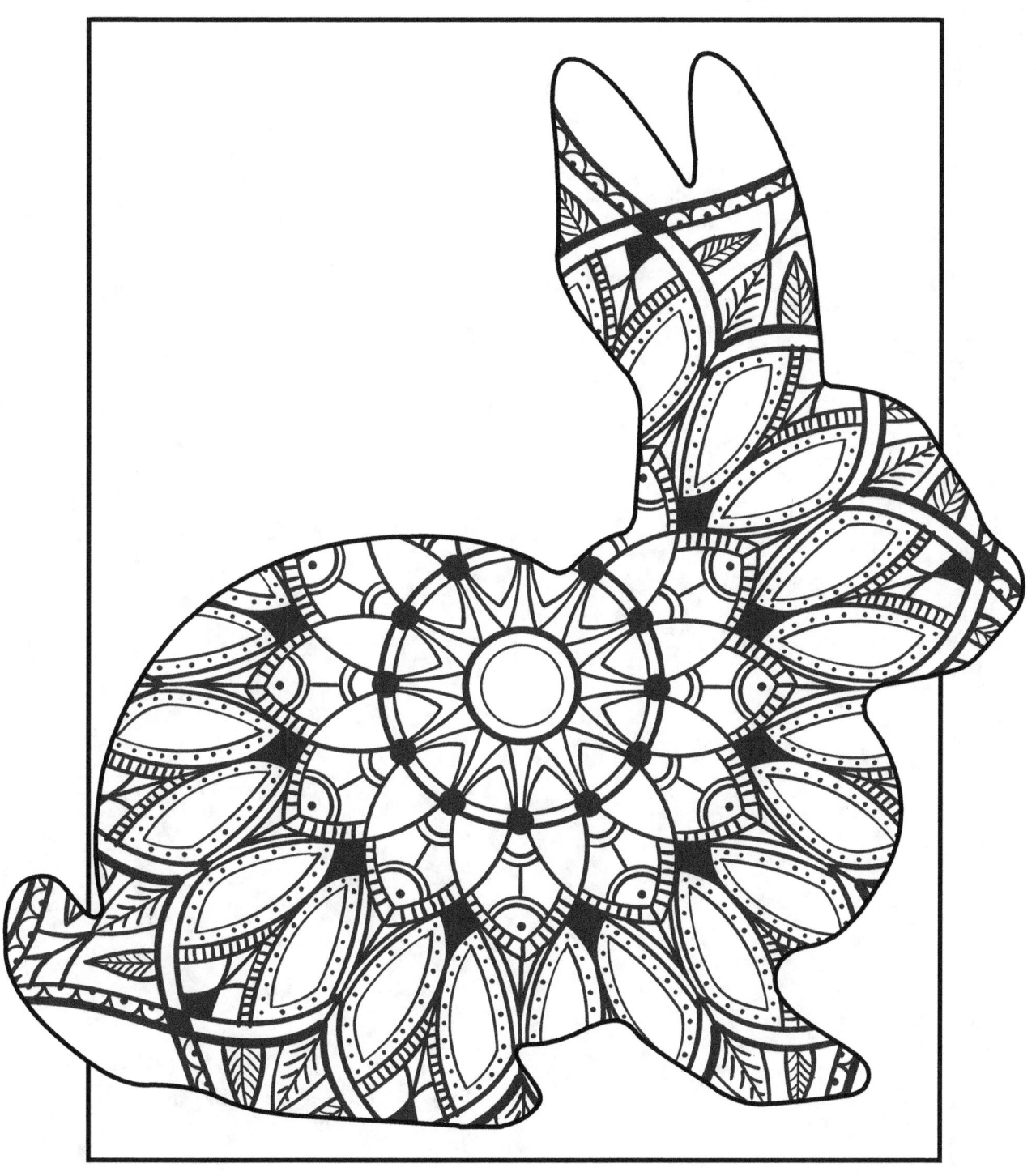

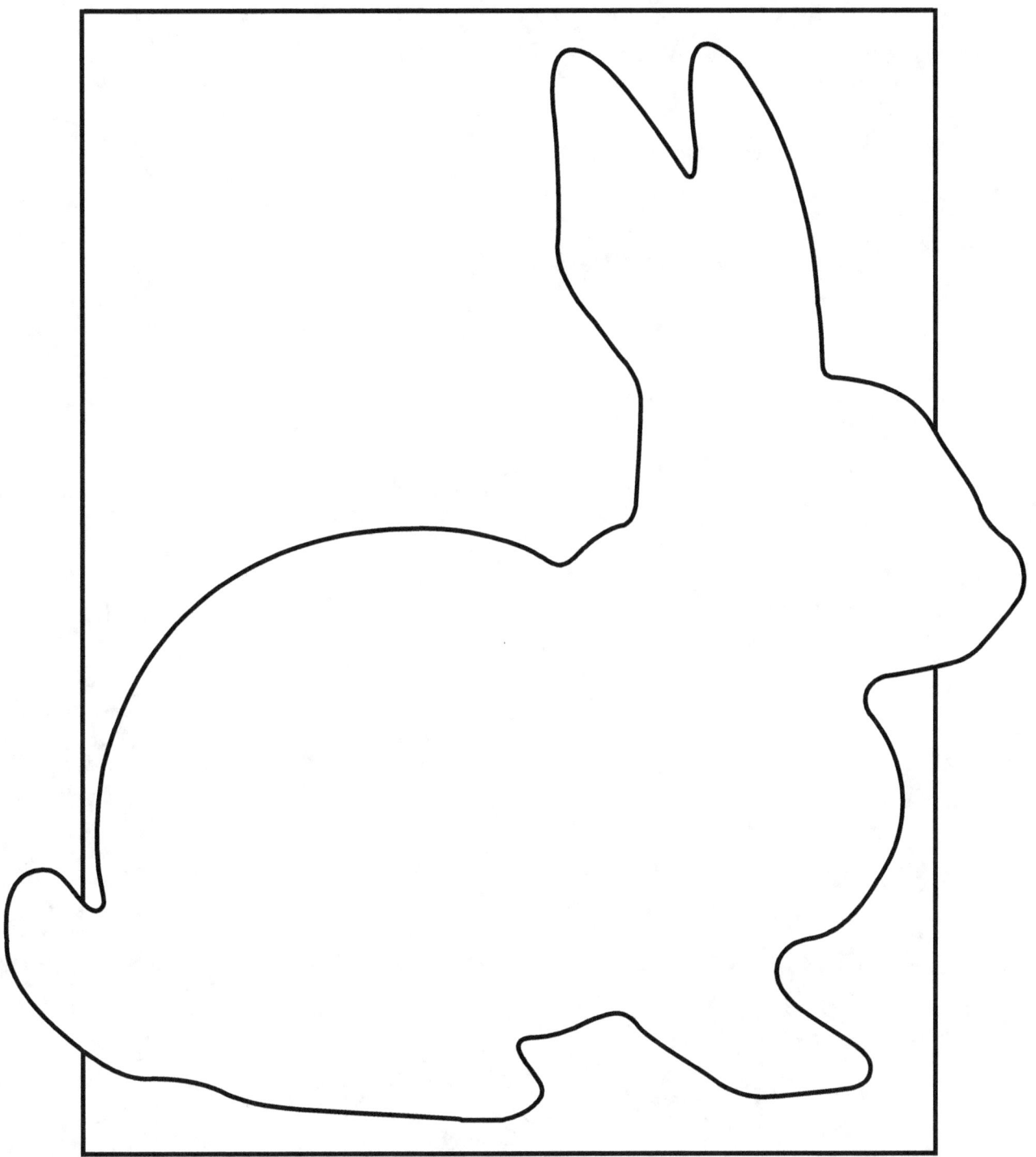

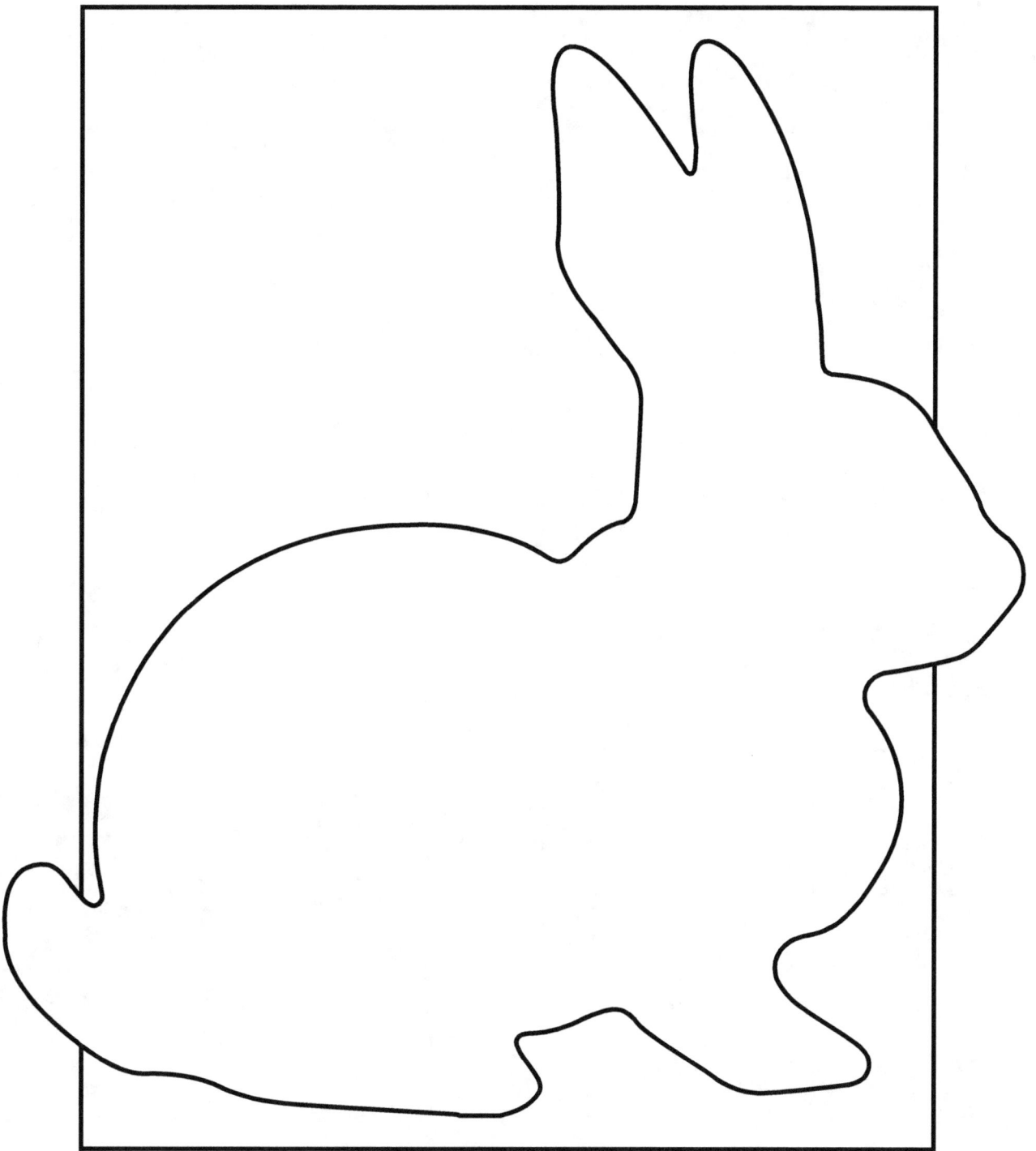

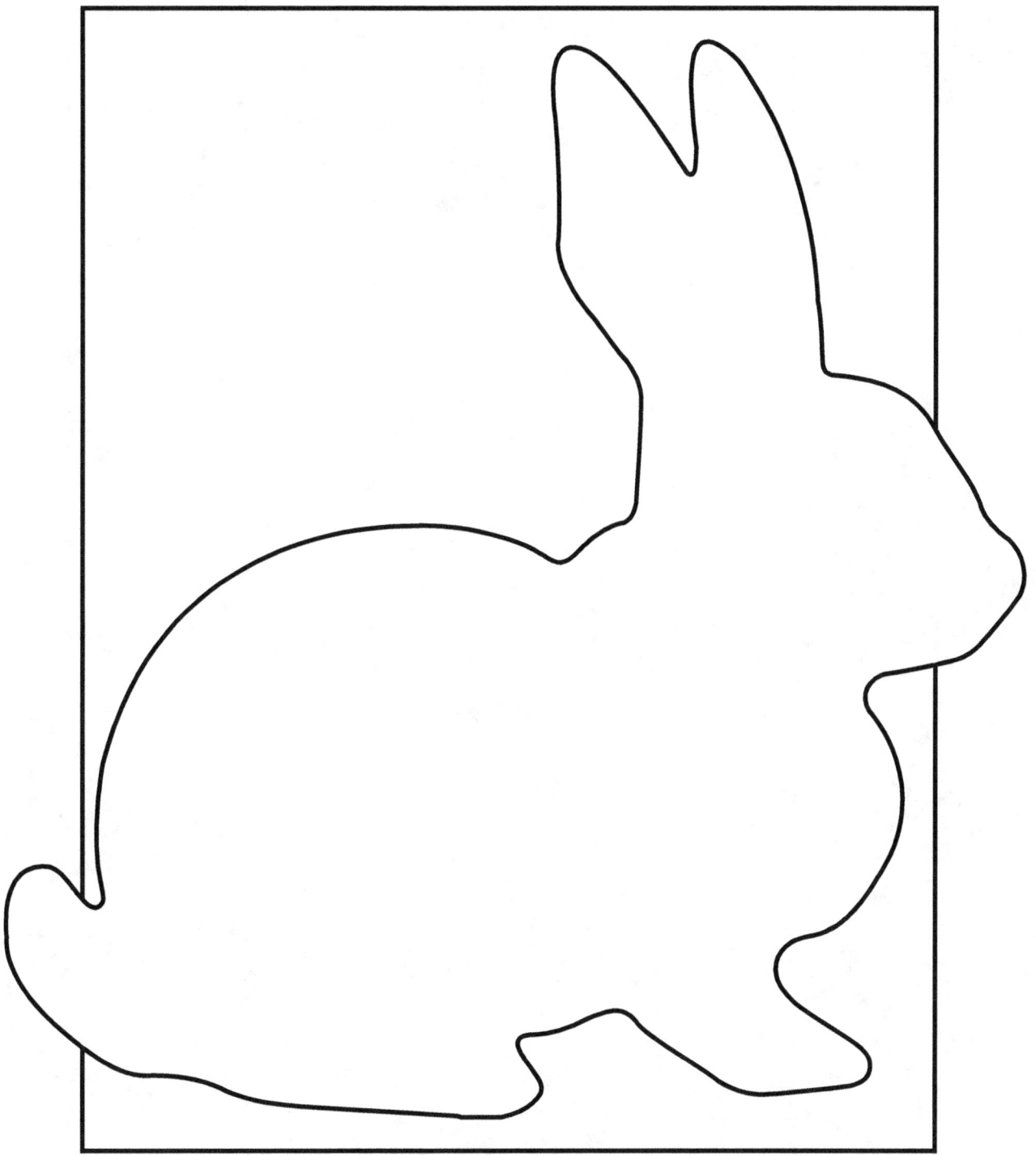

Free Coloring Sheet

AN INTRODUCTION TO DOT COLORING

Here's a unique way to relax your mind, focus and relive stress. Fill in the dots with a black marker (or a color of your choice). The halftone pattern will reveal a photographic image.
Tip: You can get an interesting duotone effect by coloring in the background with a light color and coloring in the dots with a darker color.

Was this fun to do? Please let us know at piggybackpress@gmail.com

Free Coloring Sheet

AN INTRODUCTION TO DOT COLORING

Here's a unique way to relax your mind, focus and relive stress. Fill in the dots with a black marker (or a color of your choice). The halftone pattern will reveal a photographic image.
Tip: You can get an interesting duotone effect by coloring in the background with a light color and coloring in the dots with a darker color.

Was this fun to do? Please let us know at piggybackpress@gmail.com